THE WOMEN'S CIRCLE
RITUAL HANDBOOK

WINTER EDITION

Women's Circle Ritual Handbook
Winter Edition

Copyright © 2022 by Sistership Circle

All rights reserved. No part of this publication may be reproduced, distributed, or transmitted in any form or by any means, including photocopying, recording, or other electronic or mechanical methods, without the prior written permission of the publisher, except in the case of brief quotations embodied in critical reviews and certain other noncommercial uses permitted by copyright law. For permission requests, write to the publisher, addressed "Attention: Permissions Coordinator," at the address below.

ISBN: 978-1-7351169-3-8
New Fem Publishing
email: admin@sistershipcircle.com
http://sistershipcircle.com

Cover Design: Yana Nazarenko
Layout Design: Summer Bonne
Cover Art: Katia Honour

Ordering Information:
Quantity sales. Special discounts are available on quantity purchases by corporations, associations, and others. For details, contact the publisher at the address above.

Sistership Circle International © 2022

Contents

INTRODUCTION 1
HOW TO USE THIS BOOK 2
ABOUT THE COVER ARTIST 4
WHY CIRCLE, WHY NOW 5
THE POWER OF RITUAL 7
KEY ELEMENTS TO PERFORMING SACRED RITUAL 9
SUGGESTED CIRCLE OUTLINE FORMAT 13
CULTURAL APPROPRIATION 14
ABOUT THE WINTER SEASON 16
RECIPES 24

Why I Circle 27

KAVITA RANI ARORA 28
TANYA LYNN 31
KAYLIN ELIZABETH OTERO 33
LISA MARIE GRANTHAM 35
GENIS MARIE SCHMIDTLOCK 36
LYN HUNTER 38
LEAHROSE FARBER 39
ELIZABETH JO OTTO 40
MARY SODERIOU 42

Rituals 44

The Hypnotic Orb 45
Connecting with Spider — Sinead Rochford

Solstice Family 49
Creating Winter Solstice Rituals — Ina Lukas

Release, Reflect, Reclaim 52
You are Powerful, Worthy, and Capable — Charity Murphy

New Year Visionary Mindset 55
Crafting Your Future — Chantia Thompson

Inner Womb Wisdom 58
Yoni Steam Ritual — Johanna Lee Rivera

Hekate's Gift 61
Releasing Your Burdens — Lyn Hunter

Coming Out 67
Naiies Awakening Initiation — Maria Yraceburu

Cleansing the Cauldrons with Brighid 72
Preparing for Winter — Rev. Autumn Blackwood

Celebrate the Solstice 76
Traditions for Family and Self — Genis Marie Schmidtlock

Awaken the Woman Within 83
Releasing with Courage — Kohava Howard

Elemental Aura Clearing 87
Cleanse and Bless Yourself — Benedetta Teglia

Blessing Your Words 90
New Year Journal Dedication — Benedetta Teglia

Healing your Lineage 93
Ancestral Healing with Ho'oponopono — Benedetta Teglia

The Rite of the Womb 96
Reclaiming and Blessing the Womb Space — Sistership Circle

The Gift of Love 99
Taking a Lover's Vow — **Sistership Circle**

The Garden of the Womb 103
Nurturing the Creative Cycle — **Sistership Circle**

Opening to Love 108
Cacao Self-Love Ceremony — **Sistership Circle**

Masks of Separation 111
Addressing the Sister Wound — **Sistership Circle**

Connect to Your Purpose 114
Creating Your Desire and Medicine Statements — **Sistership Circle**

Self Love Ritual 117
A Vow to Yourself — **C. Ara Campbell**

10,000 Mirrors 121
Partner Eye Gazing Ceremony — **LeahRose Farber**

Clear, Bless, and Protect 125
A Sacred Smudging Ceremony — **Syma Kharal**

Old Bones 129
Giving Your Old Stories to the Fire — **Tawny Sterios**

The Wise Woman Inside of You 133
Seeking Inner Guidance — **Snow Thorner**

Creating the Space of Sisterhood 136
Archetypal Invocation — **Ivy Rose Latchford**

Your True Self 139
Being Who You Are — **Tara Nedbalek-Mayne & Lara Kasza**

Weaving Community 142
What Does It Mean to Belong? — **Nicki Simonich & Katrina Young**

Feeling Your Intuition 146
Self-Empowerment Declaration — **Ronnie Dearlove & Stephanie Kalson**

Swirling Snowflakes 151
Clearing the Vision for Your Soul's Desires — **Cindy Scott & Carla Bonner**

Inner Jewels 155
Breaking The Box — Dulce Mendoza, Dani Hill and Maria Chowdhury

Confidence and Competence 159
The Inner Wisdom of Knowing Enough — Dulce Mendoza & Chloe Hemsworth

The Manifestation Diamond 163
Releasing to Receive — Dani Hill & Julia LoPresti

Money Stories 168
What You're (Self)Worth — Michelle Merlo & Kristin Walcott

Belonging in Sisterhood 173
The Gift of Vision — Suzanne Chenoweth and Marnae Hobson

Meeting Your Guides 176
Connect with Your Spiritual Team — Zuleimy Jaimes and Annette Bizzell

Invoking the Elements 179
Gain Clarity on Your Why — Tara Brietta and Abbegail Eason

The Anointed Goddess 184
The Art of Anointing in Sacred Circle — Chandra Nicole McAtee

Becoming the Seer 188
Unveiling Your Psychic Gifts — Emelina Holland

Invoke Your Avatar 192
Ignite Your Influence. Amplify Your Impact. — Kavita Rani Arora, Esq.

Moonblood 197
Honoring the Creative Life Force — Amy Bammel Wilding

Collective Invocation 201
Prayer for Power and Blessings — Phoenix Muranetz

Divinely Gifted 207
Discover and Activate Your Divine Gifts — Prema Lee Gurreri

Closing Prayer 211
Lisa Marie Grantham

Introduction

As more and more women rise up into their leadership and take ownership of their truth and their voice, they feel a strong pull toward being in circle with other women.

The power of women gathering is immeasurable.

And when women come together to do sacred ceremony and ritual, magic and miracles happens.

Ritual is a portal to call forth the divine.
It creates a threshold to step into something new.
It supports you in manifesting an intention.
Ritual puts feminine magic into motion.

There is more demand than supply right now so we need more women to raise their hands and be the leaders of circles, creating safe, sacred space for women to come together in sisterhood.

This handbook is designed to empower and inspire more women to lead circles using these beautiful rituals.

Many of these rituals can be done individually to invoke the divine feminine and connect deeper with oneself.

To honor and celebrate the turning of the wheel of the year, we have created a box set with four books - one for each season.

I hope you use these for your own special ceremonies, with girlfriends, or in your women's circles. Please make sure to give credit and honor the source when using them.

– Tanya Lynn

How to Use this Book

Women come to Sistership Circle to learn how to lead women's circles. They want to create safe and sacred spaces for women to connect and heal.

So we came up with the idea of compiling various rituals into these books so women have beautiful content to use in their circles.

When we asked women to contribute their rituals, some shared daily rituals that they use in their personal life. Some shared rituals they use in circle or group work.

Here's our recommended process to use this book:

OPTION A: *Use your intuition and ask Spirit to guide you.*

Go to the table of contents and scan the list of rituals and allow one to pop out and grab your attention. Or, open the book and trust that whatever page you were guided to is the ritual you should use.

Take yourself through the ritual first, using the journal prompts. Then, if you are to lead the ritual in a women's circle, use the suggested circle outline format on page 13 to craft the entire flow of the circle.

If you experience the ritual firsthand, you will feel more comfortable leading it.

We give you full permission to make the ritual your own by modifying it to your own style.

We give you full permission to make the ritual your own by modifying it to your own style.

OPTION B: *Come up with your circle theme and then browse the rituals until you find one that fits.*

If you already have a theme for your circle, or an rough draft outline and looking to insert a ritual into the flow, then read through the book until you find something that feels like a match.

Here at Sistership Circle, we focus on "talking stick" style circles, which means that we go around the circle and have each woman share on a topic.

We recommend having a potent question that everyone shares about so that you can go deep and connect intimately with one another, and then leading the ritual after to anchor an intention. After the ritual, you can get into pairs to share what you received from the ritual.

Other women choose to do the ritual first and then share their experience in the group after as part of the integration process.

The more you lead, the more confident you will become. So try different flows and see what works best for you.

About the Cover Artist

As a collaboration book, we have chosen an art piece by Katia Honour for the cover.

Katia had always been a mystic, but could barely draw a stick figure until she was 33! Trance-prayer was a normal part of her childhood, raised with the Irish Fae family working for the local Catholic monastery.

By 14, she read tarot and soon joined covens, mystery schools and spiritualist union. Ever since, she has gypsied across Europe and Asia doing social work, teaching and tarot to afford her residential seminars in Spiritualism, Alchemy, Buddhism, Hinduism, Witchcraft, Ceremonial Magick, Chaos Magick, Animist Hinduism and Ayahuasca Shamanism.

At 33, Katia was disabled in a traumatic accident and prescribed art therapy to restore neural pathways. She supplemented this with Ayahuasca shamanism and art became her way of recording each phase of the journey she was having as she healed.

"The journey of art began as meditation and re-integration for a wounded mind and body…. but I soon fell in love with the disciplines of devotional painting."

Painting helped her relax and focus. At first, she illustrated deities for altar pieces, then discovered the power of symbols and colour as visual prayers. Entering a light trance, she often channels or series to explore, observe and navigate altered states of reality.

"Nearly dying is a strange gift… it showed me how precious each breath of life is. I'm devoting this second chance to charting transcendental states with beauty, because bhakti yoga is a great way to spend my days.

Ultimately, I hope my art will invite others to explore their own relationship to Divinity."

https://katiahonour.com/

Why Circle, Why NOW

We, the spiritual women of the world, are the solution to the problem.

Jean Shinoda Bolen, author of *The Millionth Circle* and *Urgent Message From Mother* predicts that when we have millions of circles in the world, we will shift from a patriarchal society to one that is based on equality.

When women gather in circle, we transform ourselves and each other.

When we transform ourselves – when we wake up to our feminine power – we bring a new consciousness to our families and our communities.

When our families and communities become more conscious, we change society.

This is why Sistership Circle exists.

You, my dear sister, also feel this deep truth in your bones ... which is why you are here reading this handbook.

You feel the immeasurable power of the divine feminine rising as women gather in collaboration and co-creation.

> When our families and communities become more conscious, we change society.

Whatever it looks like, we are ALL being called to step into our dharma, our purpose work, and contribute our individual part to the collective healing on the planet.

What's most apparent is that we are being called to do this collaboratively, to rise up as a collective, to work together, and to unite.

It is a new paradigm of leadership - one of equality, transparency, and love.

We NEED each other. We NEED sisterhood. We NEED to rise up together.

And here's what I believe more firmly than ever: Circle is the answer to all of it.

Circle IS the new paradigm of feminine leadership.

Circle is rooted in collaboration, co-creation and connection.
Circle is the opposite of patriarchy: it is equality.

Circle is the place for us to learn, practice and embody feminine leadership.

The way I define circle is "a sacred, safe space for a group of people (more than 2) gather for transformation, healing and awakening to take place."

So circle can be a retreat, a workshop, a group program, a gathering of sisters, a gather of family, a gather of friends.

The world is aching for circle … for the connection, depth and authenticity it provides.

It's about creating more connection, more collaboration, more oneness.

We must work together to sustain the human race.

We must learn how to live together in harmony with one another and the earth.

We must embrace one another as sisters and brothers, knowing we are all interconnected. Knowing we are all one family.

The Power of Ritual

Centuries ago, it was common for women to come together in circle to support one another in birth, rest during their menstrual cycle, cook and sew together, take care of one another's children, and share stories of inspiration and triumph. Women thrived in that nurturing, connective environment where you could lean on a village sister in times of trouble and dance with a sister in times of celebration.

Over the course of history with secularization and industrialization, women lost touch with the ancient art of circling and forgot the power of the feminine.

But it's come full circle, pun intended.

Stories of triumph both collectively and personally have rippled out, touching women on all parts of the globe, creating a worldwide thirst for circle once again.

Stories like Leymah Gbowee's in her book Mighty Be Our Powers where she gathered the women in Liberia to come together in circle to protest and end a war that had ripped their country to shreds. Invoking the warrior goddesses Kali, Athena and Durga.

Or stories like mine where I spoke every week of wanting a baby and found myself pregnant within weeks of sharing that deep longing within my womb. Invoking the mother goddesses Demeter, Isis, and Ixchel.

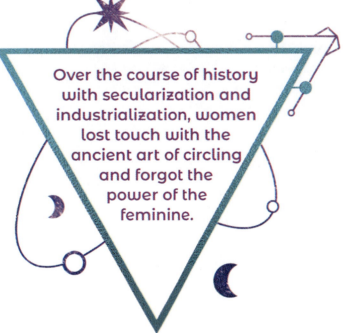

Over the course of history with secularization and industrialization, women lost touch with the ancient art of circling and forgot the power of the feminine.

What may have felt like a dream or fantasy suddenly becomes real within the collective intention of the circle.

There's something that speeds the process of manifestation up and makes the magic become tangible: it's called ritual.

According to the dictionary, RITUAL is a solemn ceremony consisting of a series of actions performed according to a prescribed order.

Rituals have been performed for centuries across all religions, cultures and traditions to bring the sacred into the mundane and manifest good fortune. A ritual can be as simple as saying a prayer every morning at the same time in front of an altar. It can be used to bring mindfulness into your day and can bring more clarity, intentionality and presence to any area of your life.

Rituals have been practiced for specific purposes throughout history in all areas of life such as to improve health, have a child, establish your power as a ruler, or become more attractive for a partner.

They have also been used in sacred women's circles to create deeper connection and manifest intentions with a group energy field.

And when women come together to do sacred ceremony and ritual, magic and miracles happens.

Key Elements to Performing Sacred Ritual

While a ritual is a set step by step process, as soon as you start to go through the motions, it loses its magic. Performing ritual is not to be taken lightly. That's why we have outlined some of the key elements to include to keep it sacred, potent and powerful.

Get Clear on Your Intention

The more clear you are on the intention of the ritual, the more powerful it becomes. With a group ritual, state the intention clearly to create an energetic field. Also allow each person to state her individual intention so she is fully invested in the process.

Prepare/Purify Yourself, the Space and the Group

Since the group's energetic field is important for ritual to maintain its magic, everything needs to be a blank slate, clear and clean for the intention to manifest. This includes making sure you come into the space clear of expectations, judgments, fears, concerns and any other baggage. The space must also be clear from other energies that were there before. The group also needs to be clear.

A purification ritual would be perfect to do for this.

This can be done through smudging (see Syma's ritual), everyone sharing anything they need to let go of to be fully present, a water purification ritual, and various other techniques.

Create the Sacred Container

The container consists of who, what, when, where, how and why. It is the masculine element of the circle that holds everyone and allows the feminine energy to be channeled. Agreements and structure create the container.

Open the container with an invocation, blessing, or lighting of a candle.

Close the container with a prayer, blowing out the candle and calling the circle "complete."

Be Open to the Mystery

The feminine is mysterious and therefore we must honor her with curiosity. As soon as we begin to compare the ritual with the last time we did it, try to control it, try to make sense of it, or want it to go a certain way, we block our receptivity channel and lose the magic.

Clear the mind, open the heart and invite in infinite possibilities. Listen. Open your physical body by not crossing your arms or guarding your heart.

Ask questions like "I wonder what is possible?"

State intentions like "I am open and receptive to what wants to come through me."

Remain Present and Honor the Sacredness

Stay with the intention and remain focused. Notice when you are drifting away or checking out and bring yourself back.

Have chatting and small talk before or after the official circle.

Maintain each woman's sovereignty, which means she is responsible for her own experience. Listen to each woman as if she has her own answers and do not try to fix or coach her.

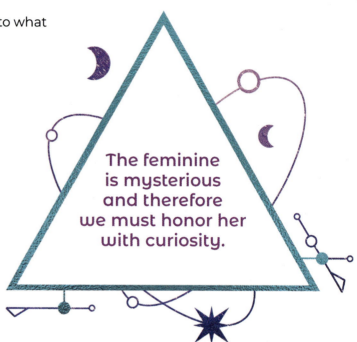

The feminine is mysterious and therefore we must honor her with curiosity.

The ritual will land differently for each woman and that is perfect. We are all on our own journeys, receiving what we need in divine timing. Trust this.

Ground and Close the Container

Because energy can be intense in a ritual, especially if it triggers something within someone, it is important to ground the energy at the end and make sure the container closes.

Ground by sharing how the ritual was or journaling, laying on the floor, using crystals or rocks in the hand, and eating something when the ritual is complete.

Close the container as suggested above.

Reflect and Embrace Change

After the ritual is as important, if not more, than the ritual itself. When you go home, take time to reflect through journaling. Practice self-care and create space for integration. Drink lots of water.

If things come up such as feeling off, triggered, emotional or disoriented, embrace this instead of resisting it. The ritual is working through you and it may take some time to integrate the change.

Creating Your Own Ritual

After reading or performing some of these rituals, you may be inspired to create your own.

Here are some of the elements of the entire circle container to consider adding to your outline:

- Prep
- Purification
- Welcome
- Opening the circle
- Invocation
- Introduction
- Ritual
- Grounding
- Reflection
- Sharing
- Gratitude
- Closing the circle
- Food
- Clean up

Here is a playsheet to help you plan:

Create Your Own Ritual Playsheet

Name of Ritual _____

My Intention is _____

Theme (Check the circles)
- ○ Full Moon
- ○ New Moon
- ○ Winter Solstice
- ○ Spring Equinox
- ○ Summer Solstice
- ○ Autumn Equinox
- ○ Blessing Ceremony
- ○ Birthday
- ○ Other

Type (Check the circles)
- ○ Purification
- ○ Healing
- ○ Connection
- ○ Journey
- ○ Meditation
- ○ Activation
- ○ Visualization
- ○ Celebration
- ○ Transformation
- ○ Manifestation
- ○ Other

Tools/Props (Check the circles)
- ○ Fire
- ○ Water
- ○ Earth
- ○ Air
- ○ Rocks/Crystals
- ○ Flowers
- ○ Wands
- ○ Incenses
- ○ Animals
- ○ Ribbon
- ○ Pens/Pencils/Markers
- ○ Paper
- ○ Oils
- ○ Music
- ○ Handouts
- ○ Cup/Chalice
- ○ Food
- ○ Herbs
- ○ Instrument
- ○ Chimes
- ○ Masks

Order
Step 1 _____ Step 3 _____ Step 5 _____
Step 2 _____ Step 4 _____

Reflection
- ○ Journaling questions _____
- ○ Paired Share questions _____
- ○ Group Share questions _____

Other Details
- ○ Who are you inviting?
- ○ How many people min and max?
- ○ Where located?
- ○ When? What time of day? What day of week? What date?

Roles (who will do what part?)
- ○ Prep
- ○ Smudging
- ○ Welcoming
- ○ Opening the circle
- ○ Invocation
- ○ Introduction
- ○ Ritual
- ○ Grounding
- ○ Reflection
- ○ Sharing
- ○ Gratitude
- ○ Closing the circle
- ○ Food
- ○ Clean up

Suggested Circle Outline Format

Opening Sacred Space
- Smudging or anointing
- Invocation/prayer
- Bringing each woman's energy into the circle

Introduction to the Circle theme and intention
- Thanking everyone for coming
- Context for the theme
- Why are you gathering

Group Share - Talking Stick Style
- Create a potent question for everyone to answer
- Use a timer to create equality in the circle

Movement
- Shift the energy
- Integrate the shares

Ritual
- Anchor in your circle theme and intention

Paired Share
- Integrate the ritual

Closing Sacred Space
- Ritual to signify the end of circle
- Announcements

Cultural Appropriation

I recently wrote an article on Blessing Ceremonies because so many women have asked me over the past three years how to create one for a friend or themselves. While doing some research, I came across an article that explained that "The Navajo have expressed that people honor their culture by not calling a non-Navajo ceremony a Blessingway, but instead to use something more appropriate like a "Mother Blessing."

This woke me up.

While I had heard of Cultural Appropriation at Burning Man, where women were asked to not wear feather headpieces because of the disrespect to Native Americans, I didn't realize how harmful we can be when we are using rituals from other cultures.

According to Wikipedia, Cultural Appropriation is a concept dealing with the adoption of the elements of a minority culture by members of the dominant culture.[2][3][4] It is distinguished from equal cultural exchange due to the presence of a colonial element and imbalance of power.[5][4] Particularly in the 21st century, cultural appropriation is often portrayed as harmful in contemporary cultures, and is claimed to be a violation of the collective intellectual property rights of the originating, minority cultures, notably indigenous cultures and those living under colonial rule.[3][6][7] Often unavoidable when multiple cultures come together, cultural appropriation can include using other cultures' cultural and religious traditions, fashion, symbols, language, and songs.[8][9][10]

While deemed "unavoidable," especially in the US where we are a melting pot of various world cultures, I believe that it is our duty, as feminine leaders, to bring awareness to this subject and educate ourselves and our circles.

This may make you uncomfortable. You may argue that you were naive and didn't think it was stealing or a big deal to wear feathers or bindis during circle. You may say that you just thought they were pretty.

If you are white like me, and not clear on your lineage, or have a "mutt" background making you a melting pot yourself, you may say, "well I resonate with the Native American culture the most because it feels more spiritual than mainstream American culture," or "I went to India and felt like I was home."

To call myself out, that's exactly what I used to say. Until I began to examine my white privilege.

This struck home for me:

Dr Adrienne Keene of Native Appropriations tells EverydayFeminism, "You are pretending to be a race that you are not and are drawing upon stereotypes to do so."

I took a course called Hard Conversations that examines white privilege and systemized racism.

And I found that Cultural Appropriation is one of the things that perpetuates racism, whether we are conscious of it or not.

So here's my point and why I am bringing forth this conversation in this book: when you are doing ritual in circle, ask yourself these questions:

Where did this ritual originate from?
Am I borrowing from a marginalized group that may feel like what I am doing is offensive?
Do I have any knowledge of this culture and the history behind this ritual?

These three questions are worth asking before doing any ritual that uses symbolism, props, music or imagery.

The same goes for using crystals, oils and other ritual items. Do you know where it comes from? Do you know the history?

Make sure you always send an intentional prayer of gratitude to and asking permission from the source of the ritual.

You can also use this prayer to begin your circles:

"We ask the permission of the traditional indigenous owners of this land upon which we sit. We pay our respects to the Elders past, present and future, offering gratitude and humility that we may sit upon this sacred land."

Rituals are to be respected, honored and revered. Lineage should be preserved. Let's make sure that we are not systematically suppressing the people whose rituals we adore through ignorance and naivety.

About the Winter Season

Yule, Dec 21

ABOUT

For people of nearly any religious background, the winter solstice is a time to gather with loved ones. Pagans and Wiccans celebrate the solstice as the Yule season, which focuses on rebirth and renewal as the sun makes its way back to the earth. Focus on this time of new beginnings with your magical workings. This sabbat welcomes in the first light as it also honors the darkest point of the year, making it potent for manifestations birthed from gratitude and the willingness to transform. Welcome light and warmth into your home and embrace the fallow season of the earth.

In pre-Christian times, people would often celebrate this holiday by lighting candles and coming together as a community around fires to encourage the sun to come back out. Everyone would bring the food they'd been saving for the winter months to enjoy as a feast and communities would get together to sing and dance. Homes were also decorated with symbols of renewal (evergreen), hope (holly), fertility (mistletoe), and protection (yule logs). Many traditions we now see and use to celebrate Christmas.

THEMES

Cave of creation
This is a time to go inward, a time to hibernate and rest. When you allow yourself to slow down, you reset your nervous system and allow the part of you that is creative to emerge. Use the Cave as a symbol for circle and create a cozy atmosphere with blankets, warm drinks, dim lights and candles, and visualizations.

Self Care
What feels soothing and good to your soul? In the slowing down, you want to be mindful of taking care of yourself, nourishing and replenishing the body, mind and spirit. Incorporate acts of self-care into your circle like foot rubs, shoulder massages, and restful meditations.

The New Dawn
The first light starts to appear at this time of year. This is a time to surrender to the mystery and unknown, to let go of the cerebral part of the brain that needs to have it all figured out. Create circles where you don't have to know anything.

Celebrating family
This is the time of year when we gather as family and community. But many times, this brings up old triggers and wounds. Create a safe space for women to share their grievances and heal the family lineage so they can feel clear and centered during the family gatherings.

Reflection
December and January are the perfect months to reflect on the year. What worked? What didn't work? What were the most value lessons? Use circle as a time to share lessons and celebrations from the past year before setting intentions.

Veil
The veil is thin during this time of year, which means that we can connect easier with the spirit world. Use a veil to symbolize this in circle, to go into the dark and connect with spirit guides, intuition and the other side.

Visioning
When we have slowed down, reflected on the past and connected with spirit, we can create inspiring visions of possibility for the future. Use vision boards, set intentions for the new year, and focus on what you desire.

RITUAL CONCEPTS

Holiday Tree: Traditionally, witches bring a fallen tree into their home and decorate with food and charms for spirits without a home to enjoy.

Welcoming the First Light: Yule is the time when the first light of the sun arrives, marking the beginning of longer days and incoming warmth.

Triple Goddess: The Maiden, Mother, and Crone archetypal-trifecta are honored as we transcend dark and light polarities in the face of seasonal death and rebirth.

> Use circle as a time to share lessons and celebrations from the past year before setting intentions.

Snow Magick: The alchemy that takes place when water turns to snow is charged with the acceptance that what is fluid is also capable of strength and sturdiness. Spending time in the snow initiates the subtle feminine into her force and ability to shift when necessary.

Cleansing: At the darkest point of the year we are given the opportunity to release all which is not in alignment for our path ahead. Utilizing smoke medicine and burying or burning all which needs to be released is tradition.

Good Tidings: Donating, giving to others, and spending quality time are all highly aligned with this sabbat. It is a time to enjoy, relax, and retreat into love as the Earth takes time away from the active force of the Sun.

SYMBOLS AND TOOLS

In Celtic mythology, the *alder tree* was symbolic of a balance between female and male principles since it possesses both female and male catkins on the same branch. The alder is a member of the birch family generally found near streams, rivers, lakes and wetlands.

In the countries around the world where *pine trees* grow, many legends, beliefs, and folklore surround this magnificent tree." Aside from representing fertility, wisdom and longevity, the pine tree is a symbol of peace

The ancient Norse used the *Yule log* in their celebration of the return of the sun at winter solstice. "Yule" came from the Norse word hweol, meaning wheel. The Norse believed that the sun was a great wheel of fire that rolled towards and then away from the earth

Evergreens were cut and brought indoors to symbolize life, rebirth and renewal. They were thought to have power over death because their green never faded, and they were used to defeat winter demons and hold back death and destruction. Because of their strength and tenacity, they were also believed to encourage the Sun's return.

Holly, which represents the masculine element, was often used to decorate doors, windows and fireplaces. Because of its prickliness it was thought to capture or ward off evil spirits before they could enter a home and cause harm. The holly leaves, symbolic of the Holly King, represent hope, while the red berries represent potency.

Mistletoe, which represents the female element, also holds much importance as it was used by Druid priests in special ceremonies during the Winter Solstice. They believed that its green leaves represented the fertility of the Mother Goddess, and its white berries, the seed of the Forest God or Oak King. Druids would harvest the mistletoe from sacred oak trees with golden scythes and maidens would gather underneath the trees to catch the falling branches, preventing them from falling to the ground; for if this happened, it was believed that all sacred energy in the plant would pour back into the earth. The branches and sprigs were then divided and distributed to be hung over doorways as protection against thunder, lightning and other evils. Mistletoe was also worn as an amulet for fertility, or hung above the headboard.

The *Yule Tree* was also another important symbol in pagan tradition. Originally, it represented the Tree of Life or the World Tree among early pagans. In ancient times it was decorated with gifts people wanted to receive from the gods. It was adorned with natural ornaments such as pinecones, berries and other fruit, as well as symbols sacred to the gods and goddess. In some holiday traditions, garlands of popcorn and berries were strung around the tree so that visiting birds could feed off the tree as well.

Candles were another way to have an eternal flame within the home. They symbolized the light and warmth of the sun and were used to chase away evils and lure back the returning sun/son.

Wreaths were also traditional in ancient times for they symbolized the wheel of the year and the completion of another cycle. They were made of evergreens and adorned with cones and berries and hung as decoration throughout the home. They were also given as gifts to symbolize the infinity of goodwill, friendship and joyfulness.

Bells were often rung during the Winter Solstice to drive away demons that surfaced during the dark time of the year. They were rung in the

morning as everyone began to wake to chase away the dark days and herald in the warmer, brighter days following the solstice.

Elves first became associated with Yule because the ancients knew that the Spirits that created the Sun inhabited the land of Elves. By including elves in the Yule celebrations, the ancients believed they were assuring the elves assistance in the coercion of the Sun to return.

Gingerbread was considered to be a specialty bread during this time since ginger had not been available until the Crusaders brought it back in the 11th century. There were strict laws regarding specialty breads in that time, so gingerbread was only allowed to be produced during the holidays and thus, it became associated with winter and Yule.

Wassail derives from the Old English words waes hael, which means "be well", "be hale" or "good health". It is a strong drink, usually a mixture of ale, honey and spices or mulled apple cider. When pagans went into the forest to fell the great oak for the Yule log, they would anoint the tree with wassail and bedeck them with wassail-soaked cakes, thus the ritual of wassailing was born. At home, the wassail would be poured into a large bowl during feast time and the host, when greeting his or her guests, would lift a drink and wish them "waes hael", to which they would reply "drinc hael", which meant "drink and be well".

Carolling was also a popular Yule tradition when young children honoured the Winter Solstice with song. They would go through the villages, singing door to door. The villagers, in return, would reward them with tokens and sweets and small gifts which symbolized the food and prosperity given by the Mother Goddess to all her Earthly children.

Nature Symbols of Yule: Holly, Oak, Mistletoe, Ivy, Evergreens, Laurel, Bayberry, Blessed Thistle, Frankincense, Pine, Sage, Yellow Cedar.

Food and Drink of Yule: Yule Log Cake, Gingerbread, Fruits, Berries, Nuts, Pork dishes, Turkey, Eggnog, Ginger Tea, Spiced Cider, Wassail

Colours of Yule: Red, Green, White, Silver, Gold

Red represents the waning Holly King. Green represents the waxing Oak King. White represents the purity and hope of new Light. Silver represents the Moon. Gold represents the Sun/Son.

Stones of Yule: Rubies, Bloodstones, Garnets, Emeralds, Diamonds

~ Originally written by Daniela Masaro. Updated/edited by Jacob Lopez Dec, 2020

https://www.sacredearthjourneys.ca/blog/traditions-and-symbols-of-yule/

Herbs

- Apples
- Bay Leaves
- Calendula Flower
- Cedar
- Chamomile
- Cinnamon
- Clove
- Frankincense
- Ginger
- Holly
- Juniper
- Mistletoe
- Myrrh
- Oak
- Orange Peel
- Nutmeg
- Pine
- Red Clover Blossoms
- Rosemary
- Rose Buds
- Sandalwood
- Spruce
- St. Johnswort (Picked at the Summer Solstice)
- White Sage
- Wild Cherry Bark

Essential Oils

- Bayberry
- Bergamot
- Cedarwood
- Chamomile
- Cinnamon
- Clove
- Frankincense
- Juniper Berry
- Lemon Balm
- Myrrh
- Pine
- Rosemary
- Rose attar
- Sandalwood
- Sweet Orange
- Spruce
- White Sage
- Wintergreen

GODDESSES

Ameratasu (Japan)
Alcyone (Greek)
Baldur (Norse) - mistletoe

Bona Dea (Roman)
Demeter (Greek)
Dionysus (Greek)

Frigga (Norse)
Spider Woman (Hopi)

GODDESS MEDICINE

The headquarters of Bona Dea, whose sanctuary is most ancient in the plebeian district of Rome, was a place where women-only rites took place. In the neighborhood of the goddess, women were given the opportunity to commune amongst the bewitchment of secrecy, sacredness, and community. Bona Dea is linked to herbal medicine, the symbology of the serpent, and facilitating the gatherings of priestesses.

On December 3rd, the Roman festival of Bona Dea is celebrated with hot apple cider and gatherings of women. As the patroness of women, Bona Dea traditions include expressing your womanhood amongst your priestess friends, uplifting each other in creativity, and invoking laughter.

The roles and mysteries of this goddess are unclear and kept to be intuitively understood. Fluidity in the way we connect with and celebrate her is the key. She is best known for her exclusiveness, as the ancient rites for her were highly taboo and even condemned by men of the time because of their secrecy. Honor your sacred feminine by creating your own ritual in the darkest part of the year on the sabbat, honoring Bona Dea when you embody your ability to lead based upon the secret chambers of your mind. The only rule is to keep your gathering secret, exclusive to your circle women, and as expressive and sexy as possible.

ARCHETYPES

Mystic - Truth, Freedom, Trust - 6th and 7th Chakra
Wise Woman - Intuition, Wisdom, Receptivity - 2nd and 6th Chakra
Queen of death - Intensity, Surrender, Darkness - 1st and 7th Chakra

MOON SIGNIFICANCE

Many women's circles are held on the Full Moon.

The moon itself is the ultimate symbol of the feminine. Her cyclical nature and ability to hold light and dark simultaneously is a testament to some of the qualities naturally inherent in all women. She is ancient, mystical and connected to a greater whole – just like you, me and all other women on the planet. This is why new moon and full moon circles are on the rise, because the feminine is rising and so many women are waking up to the gifts that women and the feminine have to offer.

The full moon represents illumination and coming out. It is a time when the moon is in its fullness in the night sky, providing us with the opportunity to express and ourselves and celebrate (especially if we find we are ovulating at this time).

The full moon is also symbolic of clarity and focusing our energy in the direction that best serves us. It is a potent time for us to charge up your energy and channel it toward manifesting the things that you want in your life.

We can utilize the magic of these moons by creating altars, doing rituals, or simply journaling to honor our most long held shadow aspects. Diving into our internal realms via meditation and creating sacred space for our feminine to be embodied is supported by the moon as she rises and shows up on even the longest and darkest nights. Circle work can include releasing the limiting thought patterns, people, places, and things that keep us in the patterns of believing we can not achieve our goals when odds seem to be against us.

The full Moon names used by The Old Farmer's Almanac come from a number of places, including Native American, Colonial American, and European sources. Traditionally, each full Moon name was applied to the entire lunar month in which it occurred, not just to the full Moon itself.

December – Cold Moon A name used by the Mohawk people, this Moon occurs when winter cold fastens its grip.
Other names that allude to the cold and snow include Drift Clearing Moon (Cree), Frost Exploding Trees Moon (Cree), Moon of the Popping Trees (Oglala), Hoar Frost Moon (Cree), Snow Moon (Haida, Cherokee), and Winter Maker Moon (Western Abenaki).

Long Night Moon is a Mohican term; Mid-Winter Moon, Lakota and Northern Ojibwe.

Other names include Moon When the Deer Shed Their [Antlers] (Dakota) and Little Spirit Moon (Anishinaabe).

January – Wolf Moon The howling of wolves was often heard at this time of year. It was traditionally thought that wolves howled due to hunger, but we now know that wolves use howls to define territory, locate pack members, reinforce social bonds, and gather for hunting. It is possible that European settlers may have used the term "Wolf Moon" even before they came to North America.
Another name for this time period was the Center Moon, from the Assiniboine people, because it was the middle of the winter season.

The Cree names of Cold Moon and Frost Exploding Moon refer to the frigid temperatures of this season, as does the Algonquin name of Freeze Up Moon. The Dakota names of Severe Moon and Hard Moon refer to the extreme cold and hard times of this season, as well as the fact that the snow sometimes develops a hard crust.

Other names for this time include Canada Goose Moon (Tlingit), Great Moon (Cree), Greetings Moon (Western Abenaki), and Spirit Moon (Ojibwe).

February – Snow Moon In the 1760s, Captain Jonathan Carver, who had visited the Naudowessie (Dakota) and others, wrote that the name used for this period was the Snow Moon, "because more snow commonly falls during this month than any other in the winter."
The Cree called this the Bald Eagle Moon or Eagle Moon. Bear Moon (Ojibwe) and Black Bear Moon (Tlingit) refer to the time when bear cubs are born. The Dakota called this the Raccoon Moon, and certain Algonquin peoples named it the Groundhog Moon. The Haida named it Goose Moon.

The Cherokee names of "Month of the Bony Moon" and "Hungry Moon" give evidence to the fact that food was hard to come by at this time.

Source: https://www.almanac.com/astronomy/moon/full

Recipes

Hot Yule Spiced Wassail

Ingredients
- 3 cups cranberry juice
- 6 cinnamon sticks
- 6 cups apple cider
- 1 orange, studded with whole cloves
- 1 apple, cored and sliced
- ½ cups brown sugar

Directions
- Simmer all ingredients in large saucepan for 3 hours
- Serve hot

Yule Log

(Bûche De Noël or Ceppo di Natale)

Serves 12 (thin slices)

adapted by Christina Conte from a McCall's Cooking School recipe

https://www.christinascucina.com/yule-log-made-easily-delicious-and/

Ingredients

Yule Log
- 6 egg whites, at room temperature
- 3/4 cup (6 oz) sugar
- 6 egg yolks
- 1/3 cup (1 1/4 oz) unsweetened cocoa, good quality
- 1 tsp vanilla extract
- pinch of salt
- confectioner's sugar

Filling
- 1 1/2 cups (12 oz) heavy cream, chilled
- 1/2 cup confectioner's sugar
- 1/4 cup unsweetened cocoa
- 2 teaspoons instant coffee powder

Mocha Buttercream Icing (optional)
- 1/4 cup (57 g) butter, room temperature
- 2.5 cups (250 g) confectioner's sugar
- 2 Tbsp unsweetened cocoa
- about 1/4 cup (1 to 2 oz) of cold, strong coffee

Directions
Preheat oven to 375°F (190°C.)

1. Prepare 15x10x1 jelly (Swiss) roll pan by buttering the pan, lining with parchment paper and then lightly butter the paper.

2. In large bowl, beat egg whites at high speed until soft peaks form when beaters are slowly lifted. Add 1/4 cup (2 oz) sugar, two tablespoons at a time, beating until stiff peaks form.

3. Using the same beaters, beat yolks at high speed, adding remaining 1/2 cup (4 oz) sugar, two tablespoons at a time, until very thick (about 4 minutes.

4. At low speed, beat in cocoa, vanilla and salt until smooth.

5. With a spatula or large spoon, gently fold cocoa mixture into egg whites just until blended (until there are no egg whites visible.) Spread evenly into pan.

6. Bake 15 minutes or until surface springs back when gently pressed.

7. Place a clean linen kitchen towel on workspace and sprinkle with confectioner's sugar, in a 15"x10" area. Turn cake out onto sugared towel and carefully peel off paper. Roll up cake, starting with the short end.

8. Continue rolling until the end, and then place seam side down onto cooling rack. Allow to cool completely. Meanwhile, prepare the filling.

Filling: place all ingredients in a bowl and beat until thick; then chill.

To assemble: unroll the cake and cover with filling to 1" from the edge.

1. Re-roll without the cloth, and place seam side down onto serving plate.

2. Cover loosely with foil and refrigerate for at least an hour before serving. This can also be frozen for up to a week, wrapped in foil.

3. Let stand at room temperature for one hour before serving.

To serve as in the original recipe: place on a serving platter, dust with confectioner's sugar and decorate with red candied cherries and green angelica leaves.

Christina's Method of Decorating a Yule Log

1. Prepare buttercream frosting: mix all the ingredients together until smooth and creamy, adding enough coffee until a smooth, spreadable consistency is reached.

2. Before placing the filled yule log on a serving plate, cut a small piece off each end of the log, at a slight angle. Cut smaller than you think you should or you'll end up with a stump.

3. Spread a little frosting on an end of each piece (outside ends) and attach it to the log to make it look like a log with two cut branches on it.

4. Frost the entire log, using a butter knife and make the frosting look like bark, by making rough streaks with the knife.

5. Alternately, you can run a fork along the entire dessert, to make it look like the bark on a log. Sprinkle with confectioner's sugar just before serving (to make it look like snow.)

6. Decorate with meringue mushrooms, pine needles, sugared cranberries, rosemary, and/or other decorations.

Why I Circle

Stories From Women Who Lead

Kavita Rani Arora

*C*ircle is in my blood. It's in my bones.

The first circle I want to speak of was actually really a spiral circle. A Starhawk Spiral Dance ritual I somehow ended up attending while in college. My first experience feeling at one with hundreds of women who were strangers at the beginning of the day, and were part of me by the end.

My brown sisters and brothers surround me in circle and song for an entire week before my wedding. Sangeet!

Never having done much of it before, it all just came back to me. I knew I had sung those same songs in times past. The ladies taunting and teasing and loving on me, the lively songs, dancing and colors. The aromas of delicious food and incense wafting through the air.

It wasn't until fall 2011 that I came back to circle again. I'd been lost for so many years and finally home to myself within circle. Before that moment, I don't even know if I'd ever really felt embodied and alive as an adult woman.

I walked into circle that day so lost, so worn, so desolate, wondering how I'd ever find my way.

As I joined my white sisters in circle, I felt myself, my presence in my body in a way I'd never felt myself before.

It was empty presence.

Presence emanating through me and connecting with the same within my sisters. Never before had I experienced such sweet love and energetic communion with other humans, and most of them were strangers.

Circle infused life back into me. It provided me with answers, new questions, whatever sustenance, or guidance I needed, a nourishing balm to my wounds from patriarchy, racism, and sexual oppression.

Archetypal, multi-dimensional healing and alchemy.

I will never be the same again. I am an evolved, magical version of myself.

I invoke not just one Avatar, but whichever one suits my fancy.

Some days, I ooze the immense love of Moksha Mama.

Others, it is a tempest of destruction and then creation, preserving, distilling truth.

Having the courage to speak up, and out.

Wielding the sword of truth, cutting clean.

The violet flame revealing the mysteries in the mastery, as it dances and jumps.

I am a matriarch, deeply supported by the masculine divine.

Moksha Mama.

Quantum Queen.

Wonder Woman

Wild Wolf Woman

Magical, Mystical Muse.

Supernatural Goddess.

Emanating iridescent rose gold love.

I am that.

You are that.

We are that.

Circle reminds us of who we are and helps us to release what needs to die.

And, that's why I circle!

A story from my Lineage

When I was little and we would sit down to pray at family Havan, my Dad would ask us what the 4 aims of life are. I would excitedly yell them out. Dharma, Artha, Kama and Moksha. Little did I know that these precious moments would turn into my lighthouse as I was navigating hurricane level storms in my inner and outer world.

4 Pillars of Prosperity:
When Divine Desire (Kama) Intersects With Divine Design (Dharma) that Is Where You Create True Wealth (Artha); And big bonus ... it's also the path towards spiritual liberation (Moksha) and elevating this reality.

Dharma – Purpose, your calling, the reason why you were born and the meaning of your life

Artha – Prosperity and wealth derived through following your soul's calling, the means to fulfill on your purpose and your desires.

Kama – Pleasure, play, delight, desire and sensual gratification

Moksha – Paradise; peace that comes from spiritual liberation; and, freedom from pain and personal reincarnation.

So where in the past money, business, spirituality, sexuality were all split and compartmentalized now they MUST come back together for true success.

Actions to take:
1. Assess where you are right now with these 4 Pillars of Prosperity
2. Tune into where you desire to be
3. Be honest with yourself about the gap
4. Journal about what you discovered
5. Set targets based on what you discovered
6. Do this planning ritual on every Solstice and Equinox!

Tanya Lynn

I will never forget the first time I fell apart in a women's circle. I had just gone through a breakup and had nowhere else to go. I walked into the house crying and fell into the lap of a sister. She stroked my face and back and held me as I cried. As the women trickled in, they all held space as I sobbed and wailed.

At some point, I stopped. "Ok, I'm ready to talk about something else now."

No one tried to fix me. No one tried to make me feel better. They simply held space for me in that vulnerable, tender moment.

Circle has held me over the years as I've gone through it all. Breakups. Getting pregnant. Getting married. Being tired and exhausted. Being pumped up and on fire. Feeling broke. Feeling wealthy.

Circle has been the place for me to bring all parts of myself and let it all hang out. A place of non-judgment. A place of acceptance. A place of love and nurturing. A place of accountability.

There are so many beautiful, profound moments of circle that have kept me committed for years. It's been a place of self-discovery, of sisterhood, of leadership, of family.

In that entire span of time, there is one particular circle that stands out as the time when I knew my deepest WHY. The reason why I was committed to being in (and leading) women's circles for the rest of my life.

It was 5 days after I gave birth to my daughter. I led circle at my house despite my exhaustion, my aches and pains, and my stitches. I gave myself permission to not lead that night, but I knew in my heart that I needed it. This would fill me up. This would give me the strength for the upcoming week. So I asked the women to come to my house instead of our typical meeting place.

I nursed my baby during that circle despite my apprehension that it was disruptive. And then at the end, we lay her down in the middle of the circle while we sang her name. Tears streamed down my face.

This is community. This is family. This is the life that my daughter is coming into.

I realized in that moment that I was in circle for her. My daughter. So she would have aunties that she could call on. So that I would be supported as I raised a daughter in this world.

So she would see what true sisterhood was like.

So she would feel comfortable gathering with her friends and talking about supporting one another instead of competing.

So she would see the power of being an authentic, vulnerable woman.

I am circling for her generation. To be the example of empowered feminine leadership. To be the example of women supporting women.

I circle for myself, yes, always. And I circle for all the women who need it. I circle and circle and circle until we are all circling. Everywhere.

One global village of empowered women and girls.

I ask you to circle with me so that together, in sisterhood, we can make a better world for our daughters. And their daughters. And their daughters.

The world needs us women to circle. To cry on each other's shoulders. To laugh and dance and sing together. To know that we are not alone. To be one.

Kaylin Elizabeth Otero

*G*rowing up, I was always very dynamic. You could find me putting on a show, singing and dancing for an audience one minute, and then retreating to my room for solitary play time the next. As a highly sensitive and empathic Being, I was tapped in at a very young age, feeling the ebbs and flows of nature on a daily basis. I felt the pain and insecurities of everyone around me, and mistook it for their judgements of my own inadequacies. Receptive and open, I was the embodiment of femininity...but I didn't know it.

I was judged, dismissed, and even shamed, especially when it came to sharing my Intuitive Knowingness. I was told I was too sensitive, too wild, too emotional, too loud, to quiet...too EVERYTHING. And so, I started doubting myself and how I showed up in the world. I tried to fit in with all the other kids and tried to please the adults in my life. I struggled with owning my power, and began seeking approval from others. I felt isolated and lost, and began to doubt myself and my Gifts.

All the people pleasing, combined with my sensitive nature and childhood traumas, led me down a road of eating disorders, addictions, promiscuity, and confusion. I HATED MYSELF and wanted to escape it at any cost.

This went on for most of my life until I found Yoga and I started to remember who I truly am. More and more, I could feel safe in my body and stay grounded in the present moment. Eventually, I decided to become a yoga teacher and began my 200 hour yoga teacher training, studying Vinyasa with phenomenal mentors. Upon graduating, I continued my studies and was blessed to spend most of my 300 hour Hatha Yoga training on the shores of Lake Atitlan, Guatemala. It was there that I had my first full on Kundalini Awakening. It was the most powerful experience I had ever had. Sitting there, speaking with the Goddess about my mission here on Earth, to assist Beings who have chosen a modern day Path of Embodied Ascension. On this beautiful island, I was also introduced to the Ancient Science of Life known as Ayurveda. I fell in Love again. I was given my next steps immediately. And so, I packed up my ENTIRE LIFE and moved, solo, across the country to the Land of Enchantment where I would study Ayurveda with yet another beloved teacher, Dr. Vasant Lad.

Having overcome addictions and an eating disorder, I began living a more sattvic and wholesome life and I felt incredibly clear. BUT, I was still not in LOVE with ME. There was a part of me who missed dancing in the club, enjoying a piece of rich, dark chocolate, or just staying up late to watch a movie. I was making myself wrong for these things based on rules I had adopted from others and fears that I would have no control over myself, landing me right back to where I was before my transformation. And while there was healing in practicing restraint, I had taken it to the extreme because, ultimately, I still didn't trust mySelf to make the right choices. I had disowned my Human and made her wrong for wanting to experience life.

That's when I had the most profound epiphany: I AM ENOUGH EXACTLY AS I AM! I AM SOUL. I AM HUMAN. I AM WILD. I AM AWAKENED. I AM AN EMBODIED GODDESS!!!

For the last decade, I have immersed my Being in Self Discovery, studying a multitude of alternative healing modalities in order to create my private practice as a Divine Feminine Teacher & Embodiment Expert, Transformational Healer, and Intuitive Guide. And although I absolutely LOVE working with women one on one, I Circle because I want these practices to be accessible to as many women as possible. I Circle because these Gifts I have been given are meant to be shared. I Circle because we are stronger together and it is time for the Wildly Divine Feminine to Rise!

Lisa Marie Grantham

Life can be so busy and distracting... so much so, that it's easy to become overwhelmed and disconnected from our dreams and desires. I have found that circling helps me to live rhythmically and with intention. In addition, I circle to connect with women in a deep and authentic way. I spent most of my life not trusting women due to being bullied as a child and teen. My defense was to isolate myself and tell myself that I was a "lone wolf". This defense mechanism worked for a while, however as I aged and did the inner work, I realized that I could not fully heal until I healed my wound around women. My truth was that I dreamed of a world where women collaborated and had each other's back. A world where women shared their wisdom, their triumphs and their deepest sorrows in non-judgement and safety... so I created that world. I birthed my program SisterMind, where I guide women on how to rhythmically and intentionally design a life that they're wildly obsessed with PLUS grow a successful online business without feeling overwhelmed or costing an arm and leg! We circle with the New Moon and Full Moon every month and tap into the spiritual and magical work of each season for both life and business. SisterMind is my safe haven to connect with like-minded women. Our virtual space is overflowing with kindness, magic, support and wisdom, it's my favorite place on earth. SisterMind is a gift to me and each of my siSTARS, and that is why I circle.

Genis Marie Schmidtlock

I circle because I enjoy sharing in community. I enjoy learning about others spiritual beliefs and practices as well as sharing my own. I enjoy the energy that is created and connected within a group of people in a circle. In being trained in the Dances of Universal Peace I have experienced the energy that can be created with a small group of people and even alone. I love the idea that singing is praying twice, dancing is praying three times and singing and dancing in community is multiplied three times by the number of people in the circle. A circle is an energetic symbol that shows connection, community and growth. We are all so lucky to be in Circle together!

My first circle was found in the Catholic Mass. Growing up I was mesmerized by the idea of the bread and wine transforming into the body and blood. I truly believed Catholic priests performed a miracle every week. As I grew older I became angry with the Catholic Church because I was not "allowed" to perform this miracle just because I was a woman.

In college I went to something spiritual everyday on campus and shortly after college I truly missed this community. When I visited my college after graduation I spoke with my mentor, a Catholic nun, and she suggested the Dances of Universal Peace. In the Dances of Universal Peace I found my home. The Dances of Universal Peace are spiritual practice in motion. Drawing on the sacred phrases, scripture, and poetry of the many spiritual traditions of the earth, the Dances blend chant, live music and evocative movement into a living experience of unity, peace and integration.

As my children were born I wanted to be able to celebrate with them. I started creating Earth Based Celebrations around the Equinox, Solstice and Cross quarter points. I believe by noticing the changes within nature, we start to notice the changes within ourselves. I would weave in the Dances of Universal Peace and other activities related to these seasons. Also I continued to incorporate communion since I feel it is such a powerful symbol that shows connection to our past, present and future as well as the importance of community. Through these seasonal celebrations I started to notice the connection to the creation of the cosmos. I created directions that interweaves the life cycles of the creation of the cosmos, the seasons, the seed and ourselves.

During this time a friend asked me to do a Croning ceremony. The two of us and one other friend did a total of 3 ceremonies. We incorporate the triple goddess--maiden, mother, and crone. Each of us received a deep healing and transformation from these ceremonies.

Once COVID hit, I turned inward like so many other people. I started doing weekly ceremonies by myself in connection to the cycles of the moon. Through this experience I was able to create my own personal ceremonies that I am now able to share with the world. My hope is to start to share monthly Full Moon Ceremonies with others in addition to the 8 Seasonal Celebrations with families.

Thank you for enjoying my creation!

Lyn Hunter

Creating balance is key for me to be able to be integral in both the light and shadow; masculine and feminine aspects of my own Divine Feminine soul. This began a new journey; my life long passion to help women go deep within and connect with their own unique feminine powers; to be all they set out to be.

For me there was only one thing missing; my own belonging. Joining Sistership Circle gives me a place to feel and to be all that I know my soul needs to be. This is a place that embraces all of my abilities and gifts so that I am able to share all that I am and all that I have to offer. Being fully embraced as a woman allows me to be able to provide a safe container and to hold space for all that are present; including myself.

"I love creating and holding space for others to feel safe" Sistership Circle has allowed me to open up and be my authentic self while embracing and embodying the woman I am. I am free to express and to be creative in my thoughts and in my ideas.

For me to be authentic means to be vulnerable and transparent in my own integrity; to be accountable in my actions. Being in circle allows me all of that without being judged or ostracized. I am loved in circle who WHO I am and never expected to be more or less; never expected to be what I am not or who others believe me to be, and I am allowed full expression of all that I am; in circle, and out of circle.

My journey began as a lost little girl. I have now blossomed into a full sexual, empowered woman who can step into her sovereignty, completely. I stand so much taller; I love so much harder and I am stepping fully into my power as a woman. I know… the work is never done. I fully embrace each of my circles as I open up to something 'more'; something else to be explored and to celebrate.

And THAT, is why I circle! "I am woman; hear me howl!"

"She Unleashed her Inner Goddess & became the Woman her Soul knew her to be" – Michelle Schaper

Leahrose Farber

As founder of the Worldwide Women's Circle, I know that empowering women shifts the global culture towards love. This journey of circle started with myself, and experiencing my wounding around women. Competition between me and my sister, fights and resentment with my mother, bullying by older girls in my high school, jealousy of my girlfriends. I carried this into my adult life: still fighting with my sister, competing with women for a guy's attention, comparing myself to my best friend, wanting to be prettier, better etc. All of this behavior left me feeling left out and not good enough. Ugh! I was totally disconnected from myself and I didn't even know it.

And then I met Mellissa Seaman. She invited me to my first Women's Circle in 2009. I really saw how much I pushed other women away. I saw that when I allowed myself to get vulnerable, that so much of the walls I had put up around the other women would melt away. I saw myself in their stories. I got to be with them in their sadness and admire their beauty. That circle, as well as every other circle since then, have been so very healing and empowering for me on so many levels. My opening up and being able to celebrate deep relationships with women allowed me to accept women for who they are. This has completely transformed my life.

Elizabeth Jo Otto

I have social anxiety. As a child through my late 20s, I was extremely shy. Making friends was difficult and traumatic. I always related better to guys than girls. I made female friendships, but they never lasted long. I craved connection with women; to have female friends, sisterhood, but it wouldn't happen. Women tended to instantly dislike me, were even hostile towards me or they didn't want intruders to their click. I was tired of being around shrewish she-devils. I wanted compassionately supportive, loving sister-friends whom I felt safe sharing my thoughts, feelings, dreams, and the deepest parts of myself with them in all aspects of life – both good and bad. Those I could be my true and authentic self around.

Around 2013, I started hearing the call to lead women's circles. I researched and tried to put something together, but life and health kept getting in the way. So I decided to focus on learning to live and celebrate my femininity: embracing my shakti and exploring creativity. Somewhere along the way, I found Tanya and Sistership Circle. It was what I was looking for so I thought, "What the hell, I'll give it a try."

I started sitting in the weekly and monthly Sistership Circles Tanya offered in early November 2016. Curiosity brought me to circle looking to meet women and find sisterhood. I found that and so much more.

I loved being in circle. I finally found a place where I belonged. I finally found connection with compassionate, supportive, loving sisters. Circle allowed me to build friendships, find hope, get healing, believe my worthiness, and build confidence. So when given the opportunity to take facilitator training, I signed up and made it happen.

On April 5, 2017, I graduated the facilitator training and joined Sistership Circle's Facilitator Tribe and have been there ever since. I knew I'd grown during the 12-week course, but didn't realize how much until Tanya, Sharlene, and some other sisters mentioned how much they enjoyed watching me blossom from socially anxious to the first to volunteer.

Through Circle and Tribe, I'm blossoming into a beautiful shakti queen. Circle is where I can step confidently into expressing my true self, unique style, and feminine leadership. I continually receive healing; with every sistership interaction, my heart opens to give and receive love, compassion, and more of myself through my gifts.

Recently my sisters have helped me through a very challenging time: a breakup where I lost my best friend, two moves within six months, a family crisis, and facing some deeply buried shadows and grief.

It's taken me years, decades even, to totally face my grief. I've been in and out of counseling since I was a high school junior. Now I'm finding ways to face, work through, and process these in my own unique way. In facing and reviewing my Trail of Grief so far…

4 grandparents
Great Aunt Thelma
Both siblings (we lost Christopher, my baby brother at 15. He'd been a nonverbal paraplegic from a drowning accident when he was 2½. Billy died from Leukemia at 46.)
Dad's cousin Elena
Our 17 month old grandchild, died from a head injury.

And countless other losses …
Buttons, my horse and love of my life, through a court battle.
2 dogs and 2 ponies – 1 that died, 1 I had to give up for the Colorado move.
2 abusive marriages and many more relationships failures.

Facing my Trail of Grief has given me clarity and shown me how loss is a huge part in my story. It revealed how important facing grief, death, and dying is to our health and well being. This insight gave direction to my circles. I realized I'm passionate about bringing a feminine, creative approach to discussing death, dying, grief, dispelling myths, and learning to live life after. I'm here to bring death, dying, and grief out of the graveyard shadows into the light of love making them un-taboo and safe to talk about.

Finding this sense of purpose, growing as a feminine leader, and finally feeling free to be my authentic self is the gift of circle. I am so grateful.

Mary Soderiou

When women gather magic happens.

Once upon a time I lived in the bush with my 'then' husband, we had three children under the age of three.

I could not drive, the nearest shopping centre was 30 minutes away, we had no close neighbours and I was totally dependent on my husband to go anywhere.

As much as I loved the 'hippy' down to earth lifestyle, the isolation really hit me after the birth of our second child.

I was hungering for women to connect with and so, quite suddenly, I decided to start my first women's circle, (or as we called it those days, a women's group). That was 32 years ago.

I had no idea what I was doing but there was never a moment's hesitation.

There were no computers filled with instant information, guidance courses or links, no Facebook, no mobile phones those days.

All I had was this desperate longing that kept guiding and nudging me.

I felt a strong inner presence that I now know as my wild and wise woman, She, who pushes us forward to know and do, 'our truth', even if it risks failing, looking vulnerable or rocking the boat.

As a woman alone in the bush with no other women close by, I was slowly perishing without the nourishment of sisterhood.

So I called the women in and the women came.

Right from our first circle where our need for tribe created a strong container that was held in intimate trust, we opened our hearts and shared in a way that none of us had ever experienced before.

To this day, I am so surprised how the divine feminine held us in all our innocence, none of us knew what to expect and yet as we sat in circle, we immediately knew we had come home without really knowing what that meant.

I could see and feel much transformation occurring for us all, the power of sisterhood was awakened. We found a place for our voices to be heard, where our vulnerability was held, where our joy could be as big and loud as it needed to be, where we could whisper our secrets to each other, where nobody judged our imperfections.

We felt expanded and able to cope with our daily lives.

We did not feel alone anymore.

As time went on, my relationship with my wild woman strengthened and I wanted to understand Her and understand what was occurring. What was this magic, this transformation, this wild creative energy within us that had been unleashed when we began to gather? As I see it now, our feminine awakening had begun and I had taken my purpose in life.

My entire life had changed as I found my voice, simply by being with women in circle.

There began a career and lifestyle that unfolded as I picked up the breadcrumbs left for me by the 'Goddess' guiding me along this journey.

I have always felt so blessed and humbled, to have the trust of so many women, to be able to hold space for them as they drop their masks, diving into the darkness of their own fears, secrets, radiating their brilliance, dancing the wild dance of 'I am'.

These women showed me how fearful I was of being vulnerable and imperfect. Their courage, radiance and trust enabled me to dive deeply into these fears and experience deep love, compassion and the power of tribe.

I am moved to tears, even as I write. Circle always leaves me filled with love for humanity. So much love, human fragility, joy and self awareness in one container that is then taken back home into our families and community.

Rituals

The Hypnotic Orb

Connecting with Spider

Intention and outcome of the ritual: to promote feelings of strength and calm as you call in the wisdom and power of Grandmother Spider

Introduction to The Hypnotic Orb:
Native American Goddess/Deity, Grandmother Spider or The Spider Woman is believed by The Hopi to have created the world using just her thoughts; the Navajo see her as a saviour for the entire Human Race and The Cherokee believe that she gave light to humanity, bringing it forth from darkness and despair.

In Hopi belief, Grandmother Spider is the Creator herself, it is with her will, power and intention that she began to consciously weave this world into creation and each one of us conscious beings into existence from her web of the vast and expansive universe.

Step by step instructions:
Begin by lighting the candle and safely placing it inside the glass jar. This represents the light of the universe, the capacity for creation, and the spark of spirit within you.

Materials and supplies: one candle in a glass jar, string or ribbon

Take a deep breath in through the nose, noticing the space between breath, the stillness and the present moment and then breathe out slowly through the mouth. Do this 3 times.

As you allow yourself to drop into your body and notice the breath, stare into the flame of the candle. Allow your eyes to soften their focus. Try not to blink. As you draw your focus into the flame, place your hands on either side of the candle, palms open and facing inward as if you are beaming it from either side.

Visualize yourself breathing love and light into your body, drawing on the energy from the candle.

Close your eyes and notice that you still see the flame and the light behind your eyes.

Focus on beaming love and light into the candle flame. Continue breathing slowly and deeply.

Repeat silently:

'Grandmother Spider, I call on you now'
'Light the flame of creativity in my soul'
'Grandmother Spider, I call on you now'
'Weave your web of creation, make me whole'
'Grandmother Spider, I call on you now'
'Awaken my passion and bless me with sight'
'May I be strong as your web, powerful yet light'
'Grandmother Spider, I call on you now'
'Bring me inspiration and flow'
'For I wish to weave'
'A world that is filled with love and ease'

Open your eyes. Pick up your ribbon and wrap it around your candle. As you do so, envision yourself weaving a new project into life. Wrap the candles and spark safely in your web of creation.

Repeat silently:

'Weave it with love'
'Weave it with ease'
'Allow it to grow deep'
'With roots like the trees'
'Bring me the strength'
'To hold it tight'
'Like the web that is you'
'Holding the day and the night'
'And so it is. And So it Shall Be'

Blessed Be.

In Hopi belief, Grandmother Spider is the Creator herself...

Gratitude Gift

The Transformation Practice free '7 days of Self Love Meditations'

https://thetransformationpractice.com.au/online-courses/selflove/

Sinead Rochford is a Clinical Hypnotherapist, Transformation Coach, NLP Practitioner, Radio Presenter and Self Love Advocate! She is based in Sydney Australia and if there is one thing she believes in this life, it is that 'pure love, energy and connecting with source is medicine for the soul, this is why circle is so powerful. The healthy and potent power of love starts with self and then expands in connection to others.' In Sinead's circles, she encourages women to discover their innate, powerful worth within, satisfying their own deepest desires, wants and needs by awakening their divine femininity through refocusing on creativity, flow, balance and intuitive awareness. Sinead is passionate about dance and often incorporates movement and embodiment into her circles to get people out of the head and back into their bodies (PS no dance skill required) Love, movement and connection are at the heart centre of Sinead's circles.

Journal Prompts: The Hypnotic Orb

What is your #1 takeaway from ritual?

What did you receive?

If you were to lead this in a women's circle, how would you make this your own?

Solstice Family

Creating Winter Solstice Rituals

Intention and outcome of the ritual:
to create a family Solstice ritual

Introduction to Solstice Family:
Raising children to be attuned to the cycles of the Earth and the flowing of the seasons, to be connected to our planet with reverence, and to honor their emotions as they cycled through the seasons of the year is potent and meaningful. Through seasonal ritual, we live in the world of magic and possibility.

Materials and supplies:
Circle Round: Raising Children in Goddess Traditions by Starhawk

Step by step instructions:
On the eve of the Winter Solstice, we are visited by Solstice Elves. My children put out empty baskets lined with silks for the Solstice Elves to come fill. We light the candles on our Yule log, and as we do we say, "We light the light through the darkest night for the Solstice Elves to find us." The Solstice Elves need to be guided by our light through that dark, dark night, and the sun needs to know that we're holding space for its rebirth. We talk about all the things we appreciate about the sun and how much abundance it brings us. When we wake up in the morning, as the sun is being reborn, the Solstice Elves have filled the baskets with appreciation for lighting the light through the darkest night. They leave us delicious natural treats from their elfin home: satsumas, nuts, dried mangoes, pomegranates.

Also on Solstice Eve, we bake Mother Winter's Wish Bread, or monkey bread, that is made from many hand-rolled balls put together in a pan. We roll each ball, setting our intentions and dreams for the new solar year to come. Those

Gratitude Gift

Winter Solstice Activation

This is a potent channeled shamanic activation that is designed to bring you through the rebirth of the sun - from the darkness into the light. Clear lifetimes of karmic debris, clarify your vision of what you want to birth, create the highest timelines though the Solstice portal, receive abundance codes, amplify your intuitive gifts, and expand into the pure potentiality of your creation. You can use this activation with your circles or your own practice.

https://wintersolsticeactivation.com/

dreams become baked into reality and savored in the morning as our wishes are sweetly released into the world.

We have a beautiful Solstice tradition of making monochromatic white flower arrangements that we place throughout the house, bringing "drifts of snow" into our home. You can use white spider mums, baby's breath, white carnations, white lilies, etc. along with eucalyptus and fun greens that create the effect of a Winter Solstice wonderland.

We have a felt star that we made for the top of our Solstice tree. One side of it is black and the other side is yellow. Leading up to the Solstice, the black side faces out, representing the darkest nights. On the morning of the Solstice, we ceremonially turn the star around so the bright yellow side faces out, celebrating the rebirth of the sun.

Reading the Solstice stories each year from Starhawk's book and creating these rituals has brought so much magic, reverence, and connection to my family, traditions that they're excited to carry on with their own children.

Ina Lukas is a shamanic channel and healer who helps people free themselves from anxiety, health issues, financial fears, parenting problems, business blocks, and more. Ina's unique approach combines playfulness and levity, with shamanic energy healing and laser-focused intuitive skills, allowing people who are ready to create a shift in their life to have fast, fun, life-changing results. Along with Janet Raftis, her quantum playmate, she is co-founder of Kairos Healers Academy, a year-long magical trade school for the healing and intuitive arts. Ina and Janet also facilitate powerful shamanic channeled activations that follow the Wheel of the Year and they lead sacred activation retreats worldwide.

www.KairosHealersAcademy.com

Journal Prompts: Solstice Family

What is your #1 takeaway from ritual?

What did you receive?

If you were to lead this in a women's circle, how would you make this your own?

Release, Reflect, Reclaim

You are Powerful, Worthy, and Capable

Introduction to Release, Reflect, Reclaim:

Intention and outcome of the ritual: to reconnect with your power

Release negativity, limiting beliefs, self sabotage, obstacles and challenges that hold you back from living your full potential. Reflect on all that is going well, all of the gifts and blessings that are present in your life. Reclaim your power to create your heart's deepest desires.

Materials and supplies: paper, pen, candle, matches, burn bowl and clearing herbs (optional)

Step by step instructions:

With eyes closed, breath deeply into your heart and meditate on what you would like to release. Feel fully into the feelings, fears, judgement and pain of the things you would like to release.

Set a timer for 10 minutes and write down everything that you would like to release. What is not working in your life? What issues keep coming up? What feels stuck or stagnant in your life? How are you holding yourself back? Keep writing and feeling into all of the feelings that come up during this part of the ritual.

When 10 minutes are up, take 3 deep breaths and feel into the feeling of releasing all that no longer serves you. Tear up your paper, burn it, or bury it.

Set a timer for 10 minutes and reflect on all that you have to be thankful for: all of the gifts you have manifested, all of the wonderful things you have in your life, large or small, grand or everyday. This part might be challenging to do for 10 minutes, but do it anyway. Feel into reflecting and receiving all that is good in your life.

When 10 minutes is up, take 3 deep breaths and feel how much you have been able to accomplish, all of the wonderful things you have been blessed with, and gratitude for it all.

Take some time to reflect on what you have released and what you have received and journal about your experience. Feel into the evidence of all that you have to be grateful for in reflection of all that you have attracted into your life. You are worthy and you are capable.

Reclaim your power as a manifestor and creator of your life. Place one hand on your heart and the other on your womb space and repeat to yourself "I am worthy. I am capable" as many times as you can, until you fully believe that you are worthy and capable. Reclaim your desires, your dreams, your goals and your wishes.

When you feel complete, take out your journal and write a reclamation statement: What are you reclaiming? When you are done, hold your reclamation statement to your heart and reclaim your power to create what your heart desires most. Take 3 deep breaths and claim your power while saying:

> I am worthy.
> I am capable.
> I am reclaiming power.

Take a deep breath and feel into your power and your desires. Claim it:

> I am worthy.
> I am capable.
> I am reclaiming power.

Take a deep breath and feel into your power and your desires. Own it:

> I am worthy.
> I am capable.
> I am reclaiming power.

Any integration tips: Journal on what it will take for you to become the woman who stands in her power and creates the life she desires. Commit to repeating your desire statement everyday and every night for the next moon. Envision what it will take for you to really take back your power and create what you are desiring. Repeat this process as many times as needed.

Charity Murphy is a Level 2 Sistership Circle Facilitator, Certified Dragontree Life Coach, Holistic Health Coach and Reiki Master. Her passion is helping women ignite the fire within....and there is no better way to do that than through the power of true sisterhood. charitymurphy.com

Journal Prompts: Release, Reflect, Reclaim

What is your #1 takeaway from ritual?

What did you receive?

If you were to lead this in a women's circle, how would you make this your own?

New Year Visionary Mindset

Crafting Your Future

Intention and outcome of the ritual: to get clear with your intentions and envision your desired outcome

Introduction to New Year Visionary Mindset:
This ritual takes you on a self reflection journey through the current year and the past for healing and forgiving. Envision more of what you want from the coming year to attract and manifest in your life. Release what no longer serves you, that is a distraction to your personal growth, that you no longer align with, and that obstructs your healing. Cleanse yourself and release it all to make space in your heart for the blessings the universe has for you.

Step by step instructions:
This ritual can be done on your own or in a circle. Adjust as needed for how many women are present.

Place the crystals on the altar or in the middle of the circle with some flowers of different colors, making a grid pointing towards each woman or yourself.

Have a space set up for food and beverages in another room or area. Light candles or incense and start the music. Set up supplies for each person where there are seats at a table and space for each person attending.

Welcome each sister with a hug as they come into your space and give them a lavender flower. After you have greeted your last guest, find your seat to start the opening ceremony. Once everyone has settled in their spaces in a circle, open with a prayer or a quotation.

Materials and supplies: crystals, flowers, incense, oil, feathers, candles, water or tea, prepared food, plates and utensils, cups, bolster or cushion, music, guided meditation, journal, pens, markers, colors pencils, poster board, magazines, newspapers, pictures, glue, scissors, stickers

Take 10 minutes to write down what you want to release and invite into their life. After the 10 minutes is up, get comfortable for the meditation. When the meditation has finished, come back to the physical space and set up for creating a vision board.

While planning your vision boards, include realistic goals, both short and long term. Add in goals for self care, family, relationships, career, and healthy habits. You are planning for the upcoming year. What do you see changing in your life? How do you get there? What steps are needed?

After boards are complete, if you are in a group, have each person share about their board.

Close out with gratitude and dedication to your vision.

Any integration tips: Keep your vision board somewhere you will see it daily.

Chantia Thompson is the owner of Good Vibz Yoga located in Michigan. I have created two impact groups, Girlz Empowered, a group for tweens and teen girls ages 8 to 17 yrs old, and S.H.E (She has Everything), a monthly women's wellness and support group where we create a brave space centered on women empowerment, yoga, meditation, and journaling. Our values within Good Vibz Yoga are to inspire, motivate, and contribute to the growth and success of all our students in class and outside of class. We promote healthy habits and consistency to help develop adults and children's personal growth for gratitude, mindfulness, and supporting roles to assist them with everyday life. When I am not working I am taking care of myself and my family. I love to collaborate and support organizations as a community partner and mentor.

Chantia is trained & certified in hatha yoga, chair yoga, children's yoga & mindfulness, yoga fitness, ganja yoga, trauma informed, breath work, diversity and inclusivity. Currently continuing education in mental health counseling, business, and meditation for adults and children. As a teacher we can never know it all so I will forever be a student to help further my education and my ability to serve others.

15% discount off anything on the site: www.goodvibzyoga.com/bookonline (code: sister15)

Journal Prompts: New Year Visionary Mindset

What is your #1 takeaway from ritual?

What did you receive?

If you were to lead this in a women's circle, how would you make this your own?

Inner Womb Wisdom

Yoni Steam Ritual

Intention and outcome of the ritual: to reconnect with your womb in a loving way and to release shame in this part of your body

Introduction to Inner Womb Wisdom:
From childbirth to menstruation, plants have always been companions to heal our wombs. A yoni steam is an ancient form of feminine care used by women in many different cultures around the world to support overall reproductive health and to access spiritual healing. Our womb is our connection to the cycles of life/death and rebirth and the seat of our creative power. When we are disconnected from our womb, we are disconnected from our intuitive knowing, from the Earth, and from accessing our full power and sovereignty.

Step by step instructions:
Set your altar space and get a warm, cozy blanket to put over your body from the waist down. Wear something warm on top and socks. The steam should gather at your pelvic area, but you also want to keep the body temperature warm.

Materials and supplies: pot for boiling water, warm blanket, low stool or pillows, healing herbs

To set up the steam, say your intentions into the water that you will use to prepare the steam. Water holds memory, so you will be supported by the ability of the water to hold your intention.

Start by boiling the water alone. Turn the stove off, then add the herbs and let them steep for 15 minutes, allowing the herbs to infuse their properties into the water and for the water to cool slightly.

While the herbs are steeping, connect with your intention to connect to your womb cave. Once the herbs have steeped, place the pot with the herbs on a rug or safe surface. Wrap yourself in the blanket from the waist down.

Sit on your low stool or kneel down with your legs on each side of the pot. Whether you are sitting or kneeling, make sure that the warm blanket is covering the pot so that there is no steam escaping on the sides. If you are kneeling, rest your arms and head to the front like in child's pose.

Check that the steam is not too hot. It should feel like a warm and comforting temperature. Stay with the steam for about 10-15 minutes.

To close the ritual, place your hands on your womb in gratitude for all the gifts that you received.

Gratitude Gift

Enjoy this free meditation to connect to your womb and the womb of the Earth to gather wisdom, support and nourishment. It might be used to accompany your yoni steam ritual, or as a stand alone meditation practice to deepen your connection to your inner womb wisdom.

wildandthemoon.earth

Yoni steam meditation
(coupon code: sistership)

Any integration tips: Journal about your experience. What images emerged? What wisdom was revealed? What actions do you desire to take from the insights of this ritual? If you feel called, make a drawing, or a poem to integrate symbols or images that emerged from this ritual.

Johanna Rivera, MPH, is a mother, artist, sound healer, community herbalist and women's health educator. She believes in a women's health approach that includes physical, emotional, and spiritual health. She mentors women to awaken their sacred womb wisdom, ground in nature's cycles, and connect to the healing power of sisterhood. She shares embodied womb wisdom in circle, workshops and 1:1 sessions. Her work is guided by deep devotion to the sacred feminine, ancient medicine and rituals and reciprocity to the Earth. Her deep desire is that women reconnect with their bodies' wisdom, their cyclic nature and to the Earth. wildandthemoon.earth

Journal Prompts: Inner Womb Wisdom

What is your #1 takeaway from ritual?

What did you receive?

If you were to lead this in a women's circle, how would you make this your own?

Hekate's Gift

Releasing Your Burdens

Intention and outcome of the ritual: to connect with Hekate's wisdom

Introduction to Hekate's Gift:
Hekate (*heck-a-tay*) is the Greek goddess associated with magic, witchcraft, necromancy, the underworld, and childbirth. She is the triple goddess of the three paths, goddess of the crossroads in both the physical and the spiritual worlds. As a Triple Goddess, Hekate rules the realms of Earth, Sea, and Sky, the conjunction of past, present, and future, as well as the Moon, the Earth, and the underworld. She is the Goddess of the Crone, the Wise Woman, and the seasons of Autumn and Winter.

Step by step instructions:
Prepare your sacred space by first sweeping your area and collecting a small amount of the debris to add it to your cauldron or burning bowl later. Smudge yourself and your area. Light the black candle and call in your Spirit Guides, Angels, and Hekate herself to assist and guide you.

Materials and supplies: journal, a black candle, a fire-proof vessel (small cauldron or bowl), a small offering for Hekate (a honey cake is traditional)

Get comfortable and allow yourself to relax. Breathe deeply to release any tensions in your body and open your heart to receive. Feel into your body by placing your left hand on your heart chakra and your right hand on your womb space. Open your heart to receive.

Breathe into the darkness of your sacred womb space, the place of creativity and life. Allow your roots to go into the ground and connect with Mother Gaia, the ancestral mother of life. Breathe her energy in and exhale the stress of your everyday life so that you may be fully present in this meditation.

As you fall into a deep relaxation, envision yourself walking along a forest path. The sun begins to descend and the darkness is rising. You're carrying a rucksack on your back. Darkness falls quickly and the sky lights up with stars. It is a new moon night and there is only the light from the stars.

You quickly become aware of the sounds of the darkness. An owl hoots in the distance and the tree frogs sing their song of the night. Your rucksack begins to get heavy. The night is lonely and cold as the seasons are changing and autumn quickly falls upon the night air. Suddenly it becomes quiet. Your rucksack feels heavier still. There is a sudden whoosh of air as the owl swoops over your head.

As you walk on, the trees reach out to one another and the path begins to narrow. The branches reach out and touch you, snagging your hair. With each step that you take, the pack on your back seems heavier than when you started on this journey. Off in the near distance, wolves howl. Unafraid, you continue along the forest path.

You hear the wolves howl again, all together and closer this time, and the pack on your back seems even heavier than before. It's now digging into your shoulders and your legs are tired and sore from this journey. You lower your head and hear the howl of the wolves once again. When you raise your head, you see that you have come to a small clearing. You stop in your tracks.

In the clearing is a woman draped in a black cloak. The hood is raised so you cannot see her face.

She is standing by a coffin. Beside her are three wolves. You are not afraid, for you know this is why you have come on this journey. She is inscribing runes into the coffin. She does not look up, but she knows you are there. Her hair is long and dark with streaks of silver.

The woman is chanting. Although you can not understand her words, they resonate in your body and you move closer to her and to the coffin. There is an aroma of yew and cypress lingering in the air, and you are mesmerized. Without looking up or stopping her chant, with a wave of her bony hand, she beckons you to come closer. You move closer to her. You can see the runes that she has inscribed into the coffin. You look up at her.

She stops her work to look at you. The wisdom and knowledge of the ancestors are reflected in her soul. She gazes intensely at you and you know she is looking into your soul. Satisfied, she nods at you and starts her chant again, drawing another rune into the coffin.

She looks intensely upon your face. "*Do you know what this is*?" she asks softly, her voice filled with power. "*I am called Hekate,*" she tells you, "*Goddess of the night. This here, is a burning coffin.*" She pauses and tilts her head at you. "*You carry something you no longer need,*" she tells you. "*Burdens which are holding you back from stepping into your fullest power.*"

"*Place these burdens into the coffin, where you can let go and surrender them to be burnt away, allowing you to be freed of them. Do you have weight? Things you no longer need, perhaps, and that are no longer useful in your life?*" she asks. "*Anger, Fear, Jealousy, Regret? Sorrow? Grief, perhaps? You have been carrying it for a long time and it is time to let them go*" she chimes.

She looks down into the coffin and chants once more as she continues inscribing runes in it. You look down at the rucksack you have been carrying, full of heavy burdens. You attempt to lift it, but it is heavier than before. You open the pack and inside are three very large rocks. Each one has an inscription on it.

You pick up the first boulder and see the word *FEAR* chiseled into it. What fear is holding you back from moving forward in your life? As you place the boulder into the coffin, you notice a lightness in your heart.

You lift up the second boulder. It has the word *ANGER* chiseled into it. What anger are you holding onto that is keeping you from being the person you need to be? Are you ready to release the anger? You look at the boulder, knowing that you can no longer hold a place for it in your heart, and you place it in the coffin.

The third boulder is the heaviest of all. You precariously lift it from the bag and see the word on the boulder. You have been carrying this one with you the longest and you are glad to see it released. What is the word you see? What have you been holding space for that you no longer need? When you are ready, you place it in the coffin and breathe a big sigh.

As your last boulder lands in the coffin, it makes a big thud. Then there is a quiet stillness in the night. Suddenly there is a whoosh as the owl flies overhead and the coffin fills with a mist. The mist swirls with a purple glow and revolves around your boulders, faster and faster. The glow turns to yellow, then orange, then red and purple again. Hekate steps forward, raises her hands over the coffin, and it bursts into flames. You take a step back, expecting the heat to singe your clothing, but there is no heat from the flame.

Breathe deeply to release any tensions in your body and open your heart to receive.

Hekate laughs; "*The fire of transformation will not harm you, child*" she explains. You stand there, fascinated, as you watch the coffin burn, and your boulders disintegrate into a pile of ashes.

Hekate steps forward with her Athame and pokes in the ashes, pushing something towards you. It is a scroll. When you pick it up and open it, you realize that this is what you have needed to move forward.

You pick up your pack – it is much lighter now – and place your gift into it. You pull something out of the pack and hand it to Hekate. This is your gift to her.

You say your good-byes and head back over to the path on whence you came. Behind you, Hekate's wolves howl, and the frogs take up their chorus once again. Your burdens have been lifted and you stride now on your path, eager to get to wherever your journey will take you.

Ahead of you, the dawn approaches on the crest of the landscape. Your soul is lighter and your heart is bursting with joy as you think about the gift the dark Goddess Hekate has given you. As you feel into the lightness of your body, focus on the gift that Hecate has given you. What is written on the scroll?

Feel into your body. Pay attention to where your body resonates most with this declaration. Focus on that resonance. What is holding you back and keeping you from achieving it? What do you need gone from your life to make it work? What is it that you need to release? Focus on that for a moment. Create an intention that will bring this to fruition.

Take out a piece of paper and write on it what is holding you back. Use the candle you lit earlier to ignite the paper and say, "I release you from my life and from myself." Drop the paper into the fireproof vessel.

Add a pinch of the debris you have collected to the fire, to represent what you are releasing from your life. Visualize what you are releasing as it is being transformed into ashes and sent out to the universe through the smoke from your fire. You are giving it back to Spirit. You are reborn in that fire. Allow the candle to completely burn down. When the candle extinguishes itself, thank your Guides, your angels, and Hekate for their support.

Gather the ashes from the burning bowl and return them to Earth, asking Mother Gaia to transmute them.

Lyn Hunter is a Certified Reiki Master/Teacher; certified aromatherapist; author and spiritual healer for more than 35 years. As a single mom; Lyn's journey started in 1994 when first diagnosed with breast cancer; a journey, with many lessons and many obstacles. Starting with a 2 year battle. That was that path that changed life. She began her journey with an intimate connection with her inner Goddess; her divine feminine. This brought her to become the healer and teacher that she is today; but that is not the end of her story. She journeyed through her pain to find purpose.

Creating balance was the key for Lyn to be able to integrate both light and shadow; masculine and feminine aspects of her own Divine Feminine soul. This began a new journey; her lifelong passion to help women go deep within and connect with their own unique feminine powers; to be all they set out to be. But one thing was missing; her own belonging. That's when she became a Master Sistership Circle Facilitator to feel a sense of belonging within circle and create safe and sacred spaces for women worldwide.

Journal Prompts: Hekate's Gift

What is your #1 takeaway from ritual?

What did you receive?

If you were to lead this in a women's circle, how would you make this your own?

Coming Out

Naiies Awakening Initiation

Intention and outcome of the ritual: to undergo purification and transition

Introduction to Coming Out: The ritual exercise itself is born of a legend about a little boy and a little girl who were lost in the forest and cared for by the Gaan, Mountain Spirits. These Grandfathers of the Directions healed the children and gave them messages to bring back to the people. The Mountain Spirits told them, "This is how the life flows!" This is Na ii es - the Coming Out. To celebrate the life transition, and to bless womyn coming into their own, the community honors, instructs, and dances them into potential. Changing Mother Earth and Spirit's power are transferred to the womyn through four stages of initiation. During the Naa ii es they reenact the journey of these first children. In turn, their life's passage is acted out to prepare them for their future.

Step by step instructions:

Stage One: Instruction & Preparation

Make an offering from your heart. An offering is a prayer made physical, a sacred craft project, if you will, and then presented to Ancestors, Land, Star Nations at the appropriate time.

Materials and supplies: journal, pen, bath/sauna, things to release

Go hiking. Take your offering and a little note pad and jot down the animals, insects, and sensations that cross your path. When you find a comfortable place, ask a question and then leave your offering. Don't worry about anyone picking it up. If they do, they are blessed. Now ask what you want to know. Sit for about 20 minutes and then return home. You can look animal meanings up online or in books. Animal knowledge can come in handy for confirmation, and it's fun to learn what your neighbors are trying to tell you. This helps us feel one with All Our Relations, safe and secure.

Sit in a talking circle with a group of friends and share your stories and thoughts on the possibilities of what you've been shown. Ask questions about the feelings that others are experiencing.

The best part is to have fun. The transition has begun, enjoy it to its fullest. This is the positive we're embracing, no negative allowed. Remember that door is closed! Now have the diligence to keep it that way.

Stage Two: Purification

The second stage is life changing. Rise at sunrise and find a gym or spa with a sauna. Bathe in the steam and relax. If they have a pool, swim afterwards. We open ourselves and fill ourselves with courage and love.

When the Purification is complete, and you are home, create a circle of stones. Space them out to make an 8 directions medicine wheel. Light a candle and put it in that circle. Let the silence come and devour you until you can hear the earth's heart, while the Star Sisters (Pleiades) pray for you in the heavens.

Stage Three: Coming Out

Feeling blissful? Your Ancestors and Totemic Guides are there with something light for you to see.

Stay in silence. After one night's rest, rise at sunrise, put some music on, and dance! Dance alone, dance with others. Then get a full body massage, maybe some hot stone therapy, and go for a walk in some beautiful nature in the afternoon. Remember to say "Thank you" a lot. All of these things open you to the courage that allows you to be loved.

Say prayers of gratitude for the messages of hope that you receive while transitioning. Silently give thanks for two things: people that believe in these ways and a moment not to move. The Naaiies is systematically designed to keep you from straying out of body too far. The reasoning behind this lies in the balancing of achieved spirit vision and grounded ability to actually manifest that vision.

Stage Four: Moments of Holiness

Are you intoxicated by the energy? At this point, it's time to go through your stuff. Doesn't matter what it is, go through it. If you haven't seen or used something in years, it's time to clean house. Make it a joyful experience.

Separate stuff into thrift store donations, things that can be given to friends and things to release otherwise. When you are done separating and tagging, smudge it all. Smudge is simply bathing something in a purifying smoke. Sandalwood is used by Hawaiians and Tibetans, Lavender by Celts and Druids, Sage and Cedar by Native Americans. Whatever you are drawn to will work.

What we believe is that in the conclusion of the Naaiies you have become an Earth Empath of Power, walking in between realities. In this moment you are Holy. Your giveaway blesses others with your sacredness and activates their own! The gift for no reason, other than love, is the blessing of infinite life.

Gratitude Gift

South: Take Your Seed, Grow Your Power

Enjoy this Medicine Wheel visualization. This video gives you Unity... the power of I am All That I Need to Be - 4:44 minutes and more available to continue your journey if you choose.

https://youtu.be/t022Q9fiUTw

When your giveaway is completed, have a party. Or have a party and do the giveaway at it. Tell of your experiences as you have engaged the Naaiies, as best as you can remember them. Be assured that it is okay if you don't remember them. The memories will return when they are needed. Also be assured that Mother Earth and the Pleiades will be there for you, should you ever need their council.

Daaiina, and so it is.

Any integration tips: Take the time to re-acclimate. The three days that follow this ritual exercise are an easing back into daily life. The energies are balanced and you are blessed with a memory of yourself and the feminine in your life that make you who you are.

Maria Yracébûrû has been creating and facilitating earth renewal ceremonies since 1964. She has been an acclaimed storyteller and teaching since 1964 and has collaborated with the Global Turn On, Daughters of the Goddess, Northern California Women's Herbal Symposium, the Four Winds Society, The Global Medicine Project, the Kanaka Moali Wahine, Regenerative Design Institute and The Heart of The Healer. In addition, Maria presents nature education, eco-psychology workshops and eco-spiritual cyclic ceremony throughout the year. She is the founder of Yraceburu EarthWisdom, visionary creator of SpiralDancing Life, and PrayerMaker for the Sedona Journal of Emergence. She has written over 25 books and is as determined to bring humans *into relationship with Earth*. www.yraceburu.org

Journal Prompts: Coming Out

What is your #1 takeaway from ritual?

What did you receive?

If you were to lead this in a women's circle, how would you make this your own?

Cleansing the Cauldrons with Brighid

Preparing for Winter

Intention and outcome of the ritual: to refresh and fortify for the winter

Introduction to Cleansing the Cauldrons with Brighid:
Brighid is goddess of hearth, home, smithing, poetry, healing, water and wells, fire, and much more. Her time is Imbolc, Mid-Winter and new beginnings. During this ritual you will connect with the 3 Cauldrons - an energy system that ties to Irish spirituality, and we will be asking Brighid to help us cleanse the cauldrons and light the heart fires to help us through the depths of winter.

Step by step instructions:
Cleanse your space physically and energetically, in whatever way is appropriate to you and your tradition. Set up your altar space with the three bowls of water and one candle behind each bowl. Do not light the candles yet.

Materials and supplies: 3 bowls filled with water (optional herbs or essential oils), 3 red or white candles, journal, pen, optional divination tool

Ground and center yourself with slow, deep cleansing breaths. As you're breathing, imagine a cauldron in your head. This is your cauldron of Knowing. Take a moment to connect to this space of wisdom, the place where your ideas are kept and grown. This cauldron is connected to the domain of Sky, of possibilities, of communication. Next, imagine a cauldron in your heart space. This is your cauldron of Motion, where your love and heart are kept. This cauldron is connected to the domain of Sea, of birth, motion, renewal. Finally, imagine a cauldron in your lower belly. This is your cauldron of Warming, where your passions, and powers of creation lie. This cauldron is connected to the domain of Land, of stability, grounded foundation.

Take a moment to breathe into all of the cauldrons. Connect to them for a moment, especially if this is your first time doing so. Take another breath here and ask Brighid to come help you with this work. You may say something like "Goddess Brighid, of hearth and home, of creation. I call to you today, to help me cleanse my cauldrons, and light my heart fires."

Pause here to welcome Brighid into your space. Hold your hands over the three bowls of water. Say out loud: "I ask that Brighid bless these wells of renewal. Brighid cleanse these waters. Brighid bless these waters."

Dip your fingers into the first bowl, and anoint your forehead. Say: "I cleanse my Cauldron of Knowing, with the healing waters of Brighid." Visualize these well waters swirling in your cauldron of Knowing, cleansing it and making it sparkle. When you feel this is complete, visualize Brighid's Hand, through your own hand, lighting the candle behind this first bowl, shining the light into the well and into your cauldron.

Repeat for the cauldron of Motion, anointing your heart space: "I cleanse my Cauldron of Motion, with the healing waters of Brighid."

Repeat for the cauldron of Warming, anointing your lower belly: "I cleanse my Cauldron of Warming, with the healing waters of Brighid."

Sit in this space of cleansing and renewal. You may journal now, ask for messages from Brighid with your divination tool, do some fire scrying and any other spellwork you might

Gratitude Gift

Ready to express yourself? Use these 10 Art Prompts. Creation is for everyone, and these prompts will give permission for your inner artist to explore through creation.

https://bit.ly/3FMACWZ

have. When finished, thank Brighid for Her time, and close down ritual space as is appropriate to you and your tradition.

You may let the candles burn down completely and offer the water in the bowls (if no essential oils) to the Earth or a houseplant. If there are herbs or essential oils, discard in a safe manner.

Any integration tips:
For the remainder of the day try to drink as much water as you can to help flush the energy body and to replenish what has been cleared away.

Rev. Autumn is an empowerment mentor that helps connect you to, and heal, your inner Child, and your inner Wild One. She is a certified life coach, a professional tarot reader, and an ordained Pagan Minister that specializes in Irish American devotional polytheism. http://www.untamedpriestess.com

Journal Prompts: Cleansing the Cauldrons with Brighid

What is your #1 takeaway from ritual?

What did you receive?

If you were to lead this in a women's circle, how would you make this your own?

Celebrate the Solstice

Traditions for Family and Self

Intention and outcome of the ritual: Connect to the Birth of the Year and what You hope to Birth in the New Year

Introduction to Celebrate the Solstice:
Winter Solstice is all about beginnings and birth as well as our connection to all of creation. It is a beautiful time to honor the coming of the light with friends, family, or on your own. Take elements of these rituals to weave into your own celebration, or follow them all.

Step by step instructions:
Create the altar. Place a cloth in the center. In the west, place a bowl of water. In the northwest, a smudge stick or matches, in the north a candle, in the northeast a rattle, in the east, a feather or fan, in the southeast, a bell, in the south, rocks, in the southwest, solstice food and drink (suggested: red berries, apples, fresh cookies, elderberry syrup). In the center, place items that are symbolic for you.

Materials and supplies: bowl of water, music, candle, rattle, feather/fan, bell, rock, 2 chalices/glasses, communion food and drink

Say out loud: "We have prepared the altar. The last step of preparation before we begin our ceremony is to transform and let go." If you are on your own, smudge yourself. If you are in a group, take turns smudging each other. Put on some music and dance for as long as you need to connect with your energy.

Call in the directions. If you are on your own, say each part out loud yourself. If you are in a group, have one person read the invocation and the rest repeat "Come join us, come help us" three times after each direction.

Begin in the West: "Feel the waters within your body. Connect with your blood and the cosmic waves all around you. Be reminded of the waters in the fall, helping the trees to let go of their leaves and prepare for the winter. Imagine the "water" waves before the cosmos was created, the waves that helped the cosmos prepare for its birth. Connect to the water within yourself and be reminded of the waters that helped us prepare for this celebration. We ask the spirits of water and preparation to come join us, come help us."

Turn to the Northwest: "Remember the transformation within your bodies. Be reminded of the transformation around Halloween. The transformation of the leaves and the ground to create soil and nutrients for the seeds to birth. Imagine the transformation that occurred before the creation of the cosmos within the womb of the parent of the cosmos. Imagine the transformation of yourself, the seeds, the earth, and the cosmos and how each transformation has its own uniqueness. Now remember the transformation that helped us in our celebration today. We ask the spirits of transformation to come join us, come help us."

Turn to the North. Light a match and candle and say: "Remember the first spark that birthed all of light into creation. The spark that sent particles and waves, light and darkness throughout the entire cosmos. The spark of the Winter Solstice is the birth of the year and brings longer days. The seed births itself into creation by sending its roots deep into the earth. You are a very special spark of birth and life. Connect with the sparks within the cosmos, the year, the seeds and yourself. We ask the spirits of light and birth to come join us, come help us."

Turn to the Northeast. Shaking the rattle, say: "Remember the sprouting of the seeds. The first sprouting of the seeds of the cosmos came together and divided numerous times, initiating the galaxies. The sprouting of the seeds occurs around Imbolc when plants start to sprout upward, animals start to stir from their long winter naps, and birds travel north for the summer. In addition, you have received many teachings in your life all of which provided the sprouting of your own seeds of wisdom to help you slowly begin to grow. Connect with the sprouting of the seeds within the cosmos, the galaxies, the earth and yourself. We ask the spirits of the sprouting of the seeds to come join us, come help us."

Turn to the East. Waving the feather or fan, say: "Feel the air embracing your body. Remember the shining star within our Milky Way galaxy. This star exploded, surrendering itself so that our solar system could be formed. The waves of this star is what connects our sun, moons and planets. The air of spring comes from the gentle breeze that helps the seeds to grow and become plants. We grow through the breath of our voice and individuality in maturity. The waves of the air around us and within us connects all of us. This connection is what helps us grow. We ask the spirits of air and growth to come join us, come help us."

Turn to the Southeast. Ring the bell and say: "Remember the partnership that is needed within the bells, two unique parts creating a new sound. Within our solar system, the sun is at the center and the third rock from that sun became our earth. On this earth, the air formed as the atmosphere embraced the planet, fire formed the core at the center, the waters formed the oceans, and the land formed the continents. Within the waters, the first seeds started to form and with the partnership of the Sun, the Moon, the Earth, and the elements, the first beings transformed to create life on this planet. Around May Day, the flowering of the plants connects two unique parts to create something new. Connect with this partnership as well as the many other partnerships in your life: your family, your friends, your pets, and all the beings on this planet and in the cosmos. We ask the spirits of partnership to come join us, come help us."

Turn to the South: "Feel yourself connected to the Earth and remember the abundance on this Earth. These first cells of partnerships came together and expanded numerous times

transforming into many different types of beings on earth. Some stayed in the waters, some took to flight, some grew from the earth while others slithered then crawled then walked upon the earth. The Earth was filled with much Abundance. Abundance can also be found around the Summer Solstice. Many of the trees and plants are in full bloom, some are still flowering, while others are turning to fruit. Connect with the abundance of all life on earth, in the cosmos and within your own life: family and friends, adventures and different parts of yourself. We ask the spirits of earth and abundance to come join us, come help us."

Turn to the Southwest. Hold up the chalice of communion food and drink and say: "Remember that many beings had to die so that others may live. All beings need food to feed themselves and come together in community so that they can continue to survive and hopefully thrive. In cultures past, around the 1st of August was the beginning of the harvest season, when the gardens started to bear fruit and could be harvested and shared with the community. Connect with the beings that came before us to provide food for our ancestors and ourselves and know that we will be the nutrients for food of future generations. We ask the spirits of communion and community to come join us, come help us."

> All beings need food to feed themselves and come together in community so that they can continue to survive and hopefully thrive.

Come to the Center and say: "Feel the solid particles beneath your feet. Feel the cosmic energy all around you. You are the connection between the particle and the wave. You are the preparation, transformation, birth, sprouting, growth, partnership, abundance, and community of all things. All things are part of us and we are part of all of them. We ask ourselves to come join us, come help us." If you are in a group, share with others a word to describe yourselves and a motion that describes you and what you hope to birth or create in the New Year. Shake your rattles to help your intentions sprout for this celebration and what you hope to birth or create in the New Year.

Many years ago, before people had houses, they would gather in caves around a fire and tell stories of what they thought was the birth of the earth and all creation. Head into a "cave" to share a story together, either a darkened place outside or inside by a fire or in a dark room lighted by candles. Read one of the following stories aloud:

Born with a Bang by Jennifer Morgan, pages 4 -16

Everything Seed by Carole Martignacco

"The Rebirth of the Sun" in Circle Round by Starhawk, Diane Baker, and Anne Hill, pages 98-100

"A Visit to Mother Winter" in Circle Round, retold by Starhawk, Diane Baker, and Anne Hill, pages 101-110

Leave each other for the rest of the day. Go on a nature walk or, if possible, walk a labyrinth. Come back together at night to share with each other what you did that today to celebrate and, if you would like, answer the following questions:

What were my experiences of the past year?
What were the most important lessons I learned?
What have I accomplished?
What do I hope to create in the upcoming year?"

At sunset, bundle up and make a grand procession outside, carrying a basket filled with figures, some evergreens, incense and tea-lights or votive candles. As the sun sets, lights stick of incense and place them in the ground nearby, then set figures in and around the cave. Say a few words about the courage it takes to shine brightly in the dark, about turning of the wheel toward light and the magic of the cosmos to bring forth the sun once more.

Now that you have shared the transformation, birth, sprouting, growth, partnership and abundance, bring the energy of this ceremony into yourselves through communion of food and drink. Sharing food during this celebration reminds us of our connection to all of creation and our community.

Close by thanking the directions. If you are on your own, say all the following out loud. If you are in a group, have one person read the gratitude and the rest say "Thank you" three times.

Begin in the Southwest: "Thank you for the food we shared here today, our community, and all our ancestors for providing food for us to survive and thrive. Thank you, thank you, thank you."

Turn to the South: "Thank you for the Abundance of the Earth, ourselves and the cosmos. Thank you, thank you, thank you."

Turn to the Southeast: "Thank you to all the partnerships in our lives: our family, our friends, the Earth, the Cosmos and ourselves. Thank you, thank you, thank you."

Turn to the East: "Thank you to the growth in our lives and the air that connects us. Thank you, thank you, thank you."

Turn to the Northeast: "Thank you to the sprouting of the seeds in the Earth, the cosmos and within us. Thank you, thank you, thank you."

Turn to the North: "Thank you to the birth of all creation, of the Earth, ourselves, and this moment. Thank you, thank you, thank you."

Turn to the Northwest: "Thank you to the transformation of the cosmos within the womb of the parent of the cosmos, and the transformation of the Earth and ourselves. Thank you, thank you, thank you."

Turn to the West: "Thank you for the preparation of the cosmos, the Earth, ourselves, and this ceremony. Thank you, thank you, thank you."

Turn to the Center: "Thank you for the preparation, transformation, birth, sprouting, growth, partnership, abundance, and community. They are all a part of us and we are a part of them. Thank you, thank you, thank you, thank you!"

Genis Marie Schmidtlock has been leading Seasonal Celebrations for over 8 years. She has taught Outdoor Education and Nature Based Spirituality to children. She is a certified Dances of Universal Peace (DUP) Leader and has been trained in teaching DUP to children. She is married with two daughters and loves witnessing their sense of wonder about nature and spirituality.

Journal Prompts: Celebrate the Solstice

What is your #1 takeaway from ritual?

What did you receive?

If you were to lead this in a women's circle, how would you make this your own?

Awaken the Woman Within

Releasing with Courage

Intention and outcome of the ritual: to let go and be free of limitations and awaken her

Introduction to Awaken the Woman Within:
The bliss of being courageous is daring without apologies or fear. It means facing your worst fear or shadow, and claiming it without feeling shame or not good enough. It takes courage to work with fear as your best friend, see it as part of who you are, see it as a lesson to grow from, and not be intimidated by it. It's loving yourself unconditionally and trusting that you have been guided. Just by doing so, you will feel confidence rising from within your soul. It's to dare to start a new thing, even if it is totally new territory.

Step by step instructions:

Find a secret place for your ritual. Sit on a comfortable pillow or mat and breathe in and out to ground yourself. Safely light your candle. Gaze into the flame and say this prayer: "I allow the wisdom of my body to guide me. I'm inviting the courageous woman within me, from the core of my being to emerge."

Materials and supplies: journal, pen, handful of natural rocks (olive sized), smudge stick or mist, candle, oracle cards

When you are ready, open your journal and answer these questions. Take your time.

> What is a burden or what is no longer serving you in your life or at work?
>
> What habits, limiting beliefs or patterns leave you feeling overwhelmed or drained?
>
> What is your biggest fear?
>
> What is your biggest challenge?
>
> What is wasting your time and energy?

Review your answers and choose only 3 challenges that you are absolutely, courageously ready to let go of. Choose 3 rocks from the ones you collected. Each rock will represent one challenge that you are letting go of.

Close your eyes, take a breath, and pick up one rock. Feel it, whisper to it, and say from within your feminine soul what you are ready to release: "This rock represents _____." Repeat with each rock.

Go for a walk in nature, accompanied by the moonlight, and mindfully let go of each rock. Say a blessing with kindness, love, and gratitude. After you let go of the rocks, sit in stillness, breathe and say these affirmations:

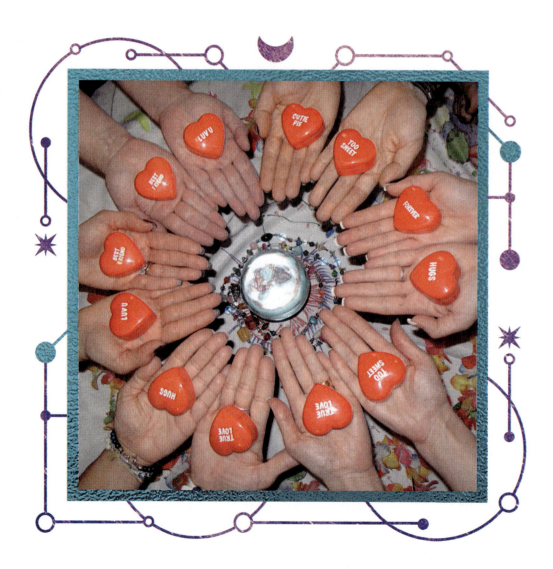

"I send love and kindness to myself. May I experience all the love and happiness in my life. May I feel protected and safe. Thank you to the past for shaping who I am today. I'm ready to manifest my life and show up fully authentic."

In your journal, courageously write down your next action step to replace and overcome the limiting beliefs, fears, and challenges that you just released with the rocks.

Ask yourself, what measures will I take today that will take me closer to my goal?

Close your eyes, shuffle your oracle cards, and choose only one message.

May you be happy, may you be loved, may you be peaceful, may you live in harmony and grace, may you feel protected and safe, may your physical body be supported with strength and health, may your life unfold smoothly with grace and ease. May you be free to live the life of your dreams.

Gratitude Gift

Self-paced 6-day guided meditation challenge, you'll receive a new guided meditation in a video format each day, right to your inbox. A journey through the Chakra system for balance and alignment. Experience affirmations, manifestation, gratitude practice, gentle body movements, breathwork, and more. These meditations will give you the power to step into a more free and vibrant version of yourself.

https://emergingvibrantwoman.vipmembervault.com/products/courses/view/1048439

Kohava Howard is an oracle, women's advocate, a mother, a wife, spiritual teacher, master healer, facilitator, visionary lightworker, holistic nurse practitioner, and women's leadership coach. The founder of Emerging Vibrant Woman and the leader of the Soul Sisterhood Collective. Her mission and passion is to mentor women empath visionaries in a spiritual awakening journey to build a courageous mindset & overcome limiting beliefs so they can unleash, courageously shine, communicate, fearlessly speak up, evolve, thrive, and flourish so they can lead a holistic life with ease. Learn more: https://emergingvibrantwoman.com/

Journal Prompts: Awaken the Woman Within

What is your #1 takeaway from ritual?

What did you receive?

If you were to lead this in a women's circle, how would you make this your own?

Elemental Aura Clearing

Cleanse and Bless Yourself

Intention and outcome of the ritual: to cleanse and bless your energy field

Introduction to Elemental Aura Clearing:
As we need physical cleaning routines, we also benefit from energy clearing practices that support us in releasing what no longer serves to make room for beautiful things to come.

Step by step instructions:
Begin by grounding and centering. Light the incense or smudge stick and say: "I cleanse and bless myself with the element of Air." Imagine a warm wind sweeping your aura, playing with your hair and clothing, swirling around you and blowing away any negative energy that you may hold in your energy field. When you feel it is done, thank the element of Air.

Light the candle and say: "I cleanse and bless myself with the element of Fire." Visualize warm flames embracing you, enveloping you and burning away whatever is stagnant in your energy field. When you feel it is done, thank the element of Fire.

Drink the glass of water and say: "I cleanse and bless myself with the element of Water." Feel a shower of cold spring water flowing down from above your head, carrying away every

Materials and supplies: incense or smudge stick, candle, glass of water, a pinch of sea salt

Visualize warm flames embracing you, enveloping you and burning away whatever is stagnant in your energy field.

unbalanced energy that you may carry in your energy field. When you feel it is done, thank the element of Water.

Place a few grains of salt on your tongue and say: "I cleanse and bless myself with the element of Earth." Sense yourself inside a shining egg-shaped quartz crystal. The stone absorbs all the energetic debris that may be in your energy field, then sinks down into the earth, carrying the stale energy with it to be transmuted. When you feel it is done, thank the element of Earth.

Think about a moment when you felt love. You may recall a memory of your past with a loved one, your friends, a beloved pet, or a moment where you watched a beautiful sunset. Feel this feeling of pure love and bliss blossoming into your heart, then allow it to expand around you, wrapping you in light and love and peace, filling your whole energy field. When you are ready say: "I am now cleansed and blessed with love and light. All is well. So be it and so it is."

Journal Prompts: Elemental Aura Clearing

What is your #1 takeaway from ritual?

What did you receive?

If you were to lead this in a women's circle, how would you make this your own?

Blessing Your Words

New Year Journal Dedication

Intention and outcome of the ritual: to bless your journal or notebook for the coming year

Introduction to Blessing Your Words:
Journaling helps us to be mindful of our experiences and is a powerful tool for growth. In blessing your journal, you are setting your intentions for the future and in so doing, gaining clarity on your goals. You may also bless a notebook you plan to use for the classes you are taking to help you focus and learn.

Step by step instructions:

Begin by stating your intentions for the next year, or, if you are blessing a notebook for a class you are going to follow, your intentions for your studies. It may be something as simple as "I choose to be open to new possibilities" or "I intend to let this class transform me in beautiful ways."

Light the incense and pass your journal over the smoke, saying: "I cleanse you and bless you."

Place the notebook on your heart and hold it close to you like you were hugging it. Infuse love into it, envisioning light flowing from your heart into the journal.

Think about your intention and try to imagine as vividly as possible how you will feel once you have achieved your goals. Let these feelings pervade you and then overflow into the journal. If you feel inspired, draw or write something on the first page of the journal. Don't think too much about it, just let your intuition guide you and pour your good feelings into the page through the pen or the colors.

Materials and supplies:

journal or notebook, pen or pencil, incense or smudge stick, optional crayons or markers

> Think about your intention and try to imagine as vividly as possible how you will feel once you have achieved your goals.

Journal Prompts: Blessing Your Words

What is your #1 takeaway from ritual?

What did you receive?

If you were to lead this in a women's circle, how would you make this your own?

Healing your Lineage

Ancestral Healing with Ho'oponopono

Intention and outcome of the ritual: to release inherited energy patterns and bring peace to your lineage

Introduction to Healing Your Lineage: Behavioural or limiting thought patterns may be an inheritance from your ancestors. Ho'oponopono is a simple and powerful technique of reconciliation and forgiveness that helps clear that ancestral energy. You can also do this ceremony simply to honour your ancestors during a Samhain Circle.

Step by step instructions:

Ground and center. State your intention: "I am here to honour and bless my beloved ancestors, as they honoured and blessed me with the gifts of love and life. I call them here with me now for this healing ceremony of love and peace."

Draw your family tree on a piece of paper. Let your intuition guide you. It doesn't matter the order in which you write the names or the places where you put them. If you don't know your ancestors' names just write "my mother's mother" or "my grandma's sister" instead. If you feel that you are struggling because of inherited dysfunctional family patterns but you don't know exactly where they come from, write in your family tree: "the person whom this procrastination comes from" or "the ancestor who started this thinking pattern."

Materials and supplies: pen and paper, optional photos or belongings of your ancestors

One by one, say the names that you wrote followed by: "I am sorry. Forgive me. Thank you. I love you."

When you finish your list of names you may add: "To all of the mothers: I am sorry, forgive me, thank you, I love you. To all of the fathers: I am sorry, forgive me, thank you, I love you. To all of the daughters: I am sorry, forgive me, thank you, I love you. To all of the sons: I am sorry, forgive me,

Gratitude Gift

My FREE Ebook "YOUR INNER MOON: Naturopathy, Womb Yoga and Sacred Feminine practices to harness the power of your cycle (even if you don't bleed anymore)"

DOWNLOAD IT HERE: www.naturalmentebeneonline.com

thank you, I love you. To all of the sisters: I am sorry, forgive me, thank you, I love you. To all of the brothers: I am sorry, forgive me, thank you, I love you."

Close the ceremony by saying: "My beloved ancestors, I honour and bless you. I am sorry, forgive me, I forgive you, I love you, thank you. Thank you for all your beautiful gifts and thank you for your presence with me. May you and I be in peace. Thank you."

Benedetta Teglia is an international Sacred Feminine coach and teacher. She is a Naturopath specialized in women's health and Women's Circle facilitator. She teaches highly sensitive women practical ways to reclaim their innate wisdom, unique gifts and inner strength and to realign with Sacred Feminine guidance so they can feel supported on their path to wholeness, achieve a greater sense of confidence in expressing their true self in a powerful and feminine way, remember the sacredness of life and view the infinite possibilities of the Universe waiting for them. She offers online: naturopathic consultations, coaching sessions, courses and workshops, Women's Circles, yoga for women and meditation classes. Learn more at www.naturalmentebeneonline.com

Journal Prompts: Healing Your Lineage

What is your #1 takeaway from ritual?

What did you receive?

If you were to lead this in a women's circle, how would you make this your own?

The Rite of the Womb

Reclaiming and Blessing the Womb Space

Intention and outcome of the ritual: to reclaim your womb and awaken its potential

Introduction to The Rite of the Womb:
The womb space is the center for our feminine essence and the home of our unique feminine power. It is the dark, mysterious void, the home to the voice of our intuition and wisdom. It is also the place where your feminine essence speaks. But many of us have not been taught to acknowledge and honour the gifts and sacredness of the womb or to listen to its unique language. Reclaiming our wombs is a journey, a kind of pilgrimage back to our birthright.

Step by step instructions:
Begin standing for this powerful womb ritual created by a lineage of women from the jungles of Peru, a lineage of women who freed themselves from suffering. This lineage of women wants us to remember:

The womb is not a place to store fear and pain; the womb is to create and give birth to life.
The feminine spirit of the jungle reminds us of this simple and vital truth:
The womb is not a place to store fear and pain; the womb is to create and give birth to life.

This lineage of women, through jungle medicine, has given us the 13th rite of the Munay-Ki: The Rite of the Womb. Once you receive it you share it with as many women as possible.

Raise your hands and summon the lineage by saying:
The womb is not a place to store fear and pain; the womb is to create and give birth to life.
Activate the rite within yourself by placing both hands over your womb and repeating:
The womb is not a place to store fear and pain; the womb is to create and give birth to life.

Transmit the wisdom from your womb to another. Turn to the sister to your left. Placing one hand on your womb and one hand on her womb space. Say the following:

The womb is not a place to store fear and pain; the womb is to create and give birth to life.

The woman receiving affirms the wisdom in her womb by saying:

The womb is not a place to store fear and pain; the womb is to create and give birth to life.

Go around until every woman in the circle has received the rite of the womb transmission.

Let us heal our wombs and those of our mothers, sisters, and daughters, and in this way bring healing to our Mother Earth.

The womb is not a place to store fear and pain; the womb is to create and give birth to life.

Sistership Circle inspires, empowers and trains women to lead women's circles. As part of our Facilitator Tribe Membership, we create monthly circle outlines. This ritual was co-created by Tanya Lynn and Sharlene Belusevic. Learn more at: http://sistershipcircle.com/become-a-facilitator

Journal Prompts: The Rite of the Womb

What is your #1 takeaway from ritual?

What did you receive?

If you were to lead this in a women's circle, how would you make this your own?

The Gift of Love

Taking a Lover's Vow

Intention and outcome of the ritual: to meet, greet and connect with the lover in you

Introduction to The Gift of Love:
The lover is able to first and foremost create that intimacy and connection with the self, and she does this through self love. She is able to see through the eyes of love and consciously chooses to fill herself up first knowing that by doing so she'll be creating more love in life. She directs love towards herself first before directing love outwards.

Step by step instructions:
Take a deep breath in and out. As you exhale, feel yourself coming back into your body and into yourself, as though you are the only one here right now, as though everything and everyone around you disappears.

Materials and supplies: paper, pen, gift box

Put both hands over your heart. As you continue to breathe, feel yourself beginning a journey into your heart. See yourself standing before you. Bow your head in love and reverence to the beautiful woman standing before you. Now see this version of yourself shrinking down, smaller and smaller, small enough that she can fit into your hands.

Lovingly stretch out your hands and pick up this little, mini version of yourself, holding her so tenderly in your hands. Move her towards your heart, nearer and nearer until as if by magic she is all of a sudden transported from your hands right into the center of your heart.

Drop all of your attention into the center of your heart. See your mini self there, completely surrounded by a beautiful pink light. Feel yourself right in the center of your heart with beautiful beams of pink light shining down softly upon you. Feel into the pure love and magic that is swirling around you. You know this is the land of the lover. Begin to walk around and take in the scenery. Notice the most beautiful frame on the wall. You feel called to walk over to take a closer look. As you get closer, you see the most dazzling, beautiful, eye-catching jewels you have ever seen, shiny and sparkly in so many magical colors. Your eyes are drawn to the center of the frame.

You realize that this is a mirror and the image staring back at you is you. Move closer and begin to stare right into your own eyes, right into the depths of your soul. Feel yourself filling up with a sense of love, awe, and reverence for the amazing soul staring back at you.

All of a sudden words flow from your mouth: "I love you [your own name]." Repeat this 3 times.

The lover in you has awakened and you feel her strong presence.

Continue looking, staring right into your eyes, and for a moment feel yourself doing a double take, because as you look at your pupils, the dark circles in your eyes, it's as though they have become love hearts. Look again and all you are seeing and feeling is love.

The lover in you has awakened and you feel her strong presence. As you look in the mirror and see your reflection, you know that the brighter you shine, the more love you feel, and the more love that you feel, the more you are able to see and appreciate the beauty in all things.

The jewels surrounding the edge of the mirror seem even more beautiful and radiant, the colors more crisp. It's as though the jewels are speaking a sacred message to you, whispering to you "The brighter you shine, the more love you create."

You get a sense that it's time to return. Taking a deep breath, invite that lover in you to come and love because she is there with you now and forever. This is her magic gateway where she can reconnect with the essence of love that she is.

When you return, wrap your arms around yourself in a loving embrace.

Take out your journal to create a vow of self-love. This is like making a pledge, a sacred contract with yourself. It is a binding agreement that compels and empowers you to choose love and to always come back to the path of love. Think of this as though you are planting the seeds of self love within your heart, and these seeds allow for your self loving beliefs and feelings to grow and develop.

As you say words and create sound, the sound vibration has the ability to affect your body and your spirit. Create your vow of self love. This is a sentence that summarises a self love vow, a promise and commitment you are willing to make to yourself. Making sure that you write it from your heart and from the stance of the lover.

If you are in circle, share and declare your vow out loud. Once you have shared it, put your vow into the gift box as you silently declare to yourself that this is one of the greatest gifts you can give to yourself and to all of your relationships.

Any integration tips: The gift you have just given to yourself is something you can come back to at any time. It is a vow that you can repeat to yourself often. The more you repeat it the more it takes away the power of any thoughts or feelings that are attuned to fear and that block out love.

Sistership Circle inspires, empowers and trains women to lead women's circles. As part of our Facilitator Tribe Membership, we create monthly circle outlines. This ritual was co-created by Tanya Lynn and Sharlene Belusevic. Learn more at: http://sistershipcircle.com/become-a-facilitator

Journal Prompts: The Gift of Love

What is your #1 takeaway from ritual?

What did you receive?

If you were to lead this in a women's circle, how would you make this your own?

The Garden of the Womb

Nurturing the Creative Cycle

Intention and outcome of the ritual: to invoke the Creatrix and unleash your creative potential

Introduction to The Garden of the Womb:
The Creatrix knows that her womb space is her power centre. She is fully embodied and allows her energy and consciousness to rest in this place. She takes care of herself, she listens to her intuition and follows her urges of doing and being. She knows what to do and when to do it. She is comfortable with both doing and being.

Step by step instructions:
Think about the womb like a garden. At first there is the rich fertile soil of darkness, the connection to the divine, to all that is. It is our link to primordial wisdom, to the place that knows and remembers all. This is the feminine in her purest form.

Materials and supplies: small glasses or chalices, a red drink (cranberry or pomegranate juice)

We will now activate our feminine essence so we can invoke and embody the Creatrix. Stand up and close your eyes. Drop your attention into your body. Bring your awareness down into your hips. Send your attention to the center point of your pelvis, your womb space (located approximately 3 inches below your navel in the centre of your body), and down your legs. Imagine a ball of light in the center of your womb space, whether you have a womb or not. What color is your light? Allow it to get brighter and brighter. Breathe into this space, with every breath allowing the light to get brighter and bigger. See this light filling your entire pelvis, your womb space and moving down both your legs. Feel the energy building. Feel your legs connected to the earth.

Imagine your legs are tree trunks and your feet are roots sinking down into the ground. Feel the strength, power and groundedness in your lower body.

Activate the energy in your hips by beginning to move your hips in a way that feels good. Tilt your hips back and forth, move them in a figure of eight, circle them around in a clockwise and anti-clockwise direction. Allow yourself to feel pleasure as you move your hips and gently bring your movement to stillness.

Know this is your powerful center, the home, the headquarters where the Creatrix resides. Take a deep breath in as we call upon and invoke the Creatrix.

From the ball of light in your womb, imagine a woman emerging. She is a woman fully connected to the mystery, wisdom, and potential of her womb. Open to the flow of life and creativity with the potential to birth anything her heart and soul desire. See this woman before you, and as you look into her eyes you see that she is you.

Place both your hands on your womb. Allow your attention to move up to your heart space. Remaining grounded, with the energy activated in your hips, take some deep cleansing breaths, softening your heart as much as possible. Imagine a loving light coming from your heart, and beam it out into the room.

When you are ready, open your eyes and allow yourself to move around the room, walking or dancing with your feminine presence and essence activated. Allow your eyes to meet your sisters, allowing yourself to feel into the powerful Creatrix you are.

Taking a seat as we explore the garden of our womb further:

Your womb is waiting to birth something incredible, a unique expression that only you can give to this wonderful world.

These are the seeds of your creativity, what you wish to create and birth in the world. With your feminine presence activated, it's time to check back into your womb and to see what seeds want to come forth. What seeds do you, today, want to plant into your womb?

This is an opportunity for you to connect to the Divine, to the Goddess, to the Goddess within you and to tune in and await for the answer to arise.

Close your eyes and drop your attention down into your heart space. Ask this powerful, wise, compassionate center to be present in this visualization. Ask it to guide you and partner with your womb. Bring your focus down through the middle of your body, along your spine, all the way down into your womb space. This is the space where we can activate your intuition.

Ask permission from your womb that it may work together with your heart to open you and to guide you to your intuitive forces within. See light from your heart traveling down and merging with the light in your womb space. Ask your heart and womb to open you to your creative potential. Open yourself up to what wants to come through and be birthed by you now.

Ask the question, "What does the Creatrix in me want to birth right now?" Trust and allow the answers to come.

Give thanks to your heart and womb for whatever they have shared with you. Even if nothing came to you, give thanks, knowing that there is a reason for everything.

These first parts of our garden are mostly about us being open to receiving whatever wants to come through. Now it's time to move into the more masculine part, the part of the creation cycle where there is movement, where we begin to play our part in the active manifestation of our dreams, desires, and downloads.

Give thanks to your heart and womb for whatever they have shared with you.

Take your womb cup, your sacred chalice that is symbolically filled with the sacred inner waters of your womb. Inside is the liquid that nourishes and sustains life. A symbol of the inner waters of our womb surrounding a growing child, now a symbol of life giving nourishment and protection for your own seeds of creation.

Hold the chalice in your hands next to your womb space. Close your eyes and tune into the seeds you wish to plant in your sacred garden. See yourself in the garden of your womb, planting the seeds in the soil. One by one, carefully plant your seeds. With your seeds planted, bring your chalice to your heart. Tune in again to the seeds you have planted, feeling your heart and the sacred chalice between your hands.

When you are ready, slowly and purposefully bring the sacred chalice to your lips and drink from it. As you do, see yourself watering your seeds, nourishing them with this life giving liquid. See yourself holding the sacred chalice in your garden and pouring this over the seeds you have just planted. As you swallow, feel the water as liquid light, traveling all the way down into your womb, watering the seeds you have planted there.

If those seeds were to sprout, what would they need from you to keep growing? What action would you need to take? How would you water them?

Come together in co-creation to birth a piece of art which will be a reflection of our creative power. In circle, invite the Creatrix in all of us to come out to play. Tune into your own seeds. What would it look like once your seeds flower and bloom? See the physical manifestation of the seeds you planted, your garden blossoming and blooming.

Put on some music, dance, and co-create by painting on a shared canvas. Keep coming back to your womb, grounding yourself as you listen to the music and open yourself up to whatever wants to flow through you. See your womb garden beginning to sprout, the shoots poking up through the earth.

What fruits will you reap once your seeds have fully grown and blossomed into their full physical manifestation? Who will benefit and enjoy these fruits?

See yourself in your garden, now picking and enjoying the fruits.

Two women at a time go to the canvas, adding their expression of their fruits. What do your fruits look like?

Reveal the group painting as you celebrate the Creatrix in everyone. Every woman has the power and ability to create, no matter how she may judge or criticise what she perceives to be her creative ability. Celebrate your group creation and the power that women have to create and birth.

Sistership Circle inspires, empowers and trains women to lead women's circles. As part of our Facilitator Tribe Membership, we create monthly circle outlines. This ritual was co-created by Tanya Lynn and other advanced facilitators. http://sistershipcircle.com/become-a-facilitator

Journal Prompts: The Garden of the Womb

What is your #1 takeaway from ritual?

What did you receive?

If you were to lead this in a women's circle, how would you make this your own?

Opening to Love

Cacao Self-Love Ceremony

Intention and outcome of the ritual: to awaken intuition, inner vision, and truth

Introduction to Opening to Love:
This ceremony supports us in creating a sacred space, so that we can deeply open our hearts and open to the healing medicine of cacao.

Step by step instructions:
Consider the following questions:
What is getting in the way of you loving yourself?
What are you missing out on by not giving regular love to yourself?

Materials and supplies: cacao, mug, music, an offering to cacao for the altar

This ritual can be done on your own or in circle. If you are on your own, reverently pour cacao for yourself. If you are in circle, designate one person to pour or have each sister pour for the next.

Once everyone has some cacao, play this song:

https://www.youtube.com/watch?v=JNoFkWIhcxo&list=PLwHBIhmhdQb3MujoXQ_wWjuwQDvoQiRR6&index=10

It is time to call forth the potent power of cacao. She is a sacred plant medicine who can guide us to receiving exactly what we need.

May the spirit of cacao guide us inwards and help us in processing negative emotions and healing old wounds.

May she guide us to restoring our vital energy as we remove glocks and gain clearer visions of the next steps we need.

Give your offering to the sacred spirit of cacao, with love and gratitude. Place your offerings to cacao on the altar.

Take in this medicine and surrender to the guidance and wisdom she will bring:

Raise your mug to your heart, over your heart chakras, as you give gratitude and open your hearts.

Raise your mug to your third eye as you call forth wisdom and divine guidance.

Any integration tips:
Drink plenty of water during and after the ceremony as cacao can have a strongly detoxifying effect on the body. You may want to ground your energy more after the ceremony by eating some nourishing and healthy food.

You may also notice that feelings and insights arise afterwards. This is normal. They are coming up to be processed and integrated. You might want to take some time to find some quite reflective space and journal which can help you work with the realizations that come through.

Take time to drink, relax, and enjoy in silence as you allow yourself to open to the medicine of this sacred plant. Tune into your heart and ask, what are some of the ways in which you can begin indulging in self love? What does this look like for you? What does it feel like?

Put on some music and dance in celebration of self-love.

Sistership Circle inspires, empowers and trains women to lead women's circles. As part of our Facilitator Tribe Membership, we create monthly circle outlines. This ritual was co-created by Tanya Lynn and Natasha Daubney. Learn more at: http://sistershipcircle.com/become-a-facilitator

Journal Prompts: Opening to Love

What is your #1 takeaway from ritual?

What did you receive?

If you were to lead this in a women's circle, how would you make this your own?

Masks of Separation

Addressing the Sister Wound

Intention and outcome of the ritual: to remove our masks of separation

Introduction to Masks of Separation:
The sisterhood wound is the trauma, pain, and fear that keeps the feminine shut down and prevents women from experiencing real, authentic, and sacred sisterhood. It is ancestral trauma which is passed on and handed down. Within the collective, women as a whole feel and know this wounding. The sisterhood wound can show up basically wherever we have relationships with other women. As we go about our day to day lives, trying to protect and defend ourselves, the sisterhood wound continues, and we miss out on the experience of real, authentic, sacred sisterhood.

Step by step instructions:
Tune into what it is that keeps you feeling disconnected from other women. Take a paper plate and begin to write those words on the front of the plate.

Materials and supplies: paper plate, pens or markers

When you have finished, choose a sister and hand your plate to her.

The plate now becomes a mask: the mask of the sisterhood wound. The mask that keeps us disconnected and separated from each other, from other women and from the feminine.

Hold the plate up to your face and turn to face your sister, who will now represent a mirror reflecting back to you the sisterhood wounds that keep us separated and disconnected.

Take turns reading to your sister the words you see on her mask. She will do the same.

As you hear those words, can you allow yourself to open your heart and really feel the separation and disconnection?

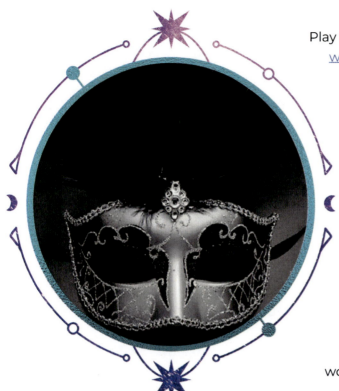

Play this music: https://www.youtube.com/watch?v=vC3DaSfrjFQ and begin to walk slowly around the room amongst one another. When the music stops, find the nearest sister to you and, all at the same time, begin to shout out the words you see written on the mask in front of you.

Play the music again and again, repeating this process.

When it is complete, consider these questions:
How did that exercise make you feel?
How does it feel to witness and acknowledge all that separation?
What is most alive for you around the sisterhood wound?

Play this song: https://www.youtube.com/watch?v=WbN0nX61rIs and shake out all the separation and disconnection.

Sistership Circle inspires, empowers and trains women to lead women's circles. As part of our Facilitator Tribe Membership, we create monthly circle outlines. This ritual was co-created by Tanya Lynn and other advanced facilitators. http://sistershipcircle.com/become-a-facilitator

Journal Prompts: Masks of Separation

What is your #1 takeaway from ritual?

What did you receive?

If you were to lead this in a women's circle, how would you make this your own?

Connect to Your Purpose

Creating Your Desire and Medicine Statements

Intention and outcome of the ritual: to create a desire statement to help you achieve and manifest in the coming year

Introduction to Connect to Your Purpose:
Desire and medicine statements are so powerful because they can help us to embody the energy, feelings and vibration we want to attract, and it helps you to attract what it is you desire into your life.

This is really supporting us on an energetic level as we are, in every moment, creating our reality by whatever we are thinking and embodying.

Step by step instructions:
Write down your desire statement using present tense and the following format:

[Your Name] is experiencing _____.

Materials and supplies: pen, paper, and an object that represents your desire

Write down your medicine statement. What medicine do you want to offer the world, your family, and your community?

[Your Name] is _____ to _____.

Show your object to the group. State your desire statement and medicine statement. As you do so, send energy into your object. The rest of the women will hold you as you share, will visualize you in your statements, and will send energy into the object you are holding. When you are complete, say "And so it is!"

Close your eyes. With your object(s) in your hand, tune into your vision, your word, your desire and medicine statements. This is your sacred contract for the year and the object you are now holding is a symbol of your contract. Pull the object close to your heart, knowing that within you lies the power and the potency to create your heart's deepest desires and visions.

Remember no one can do what you do the way you do. What you do is needed and wanted. You have a unique purpose that has always lived within you. This purpose will continue to call on you until you say yes!

Remember saying yes will call upon you to become more than you are. This is the bliss of life, to be the most you that you can be. The key is to keep going no matter what. You can start and stop as many times as you need to.

Remember that unless you do this you may always wonder, "What If?" To try to live a dream changes how we dream, even if we don't reach it. Living a dream, is the journey, is the process, is the dream revealing itself. We are not waiting for a destination, since we can live each moment truly.

Remember it will sometimes seem as if forces are against you. When we gather up enough speed to break through the resistances, we often encounter obstacles. This is not a sign to turn back. When we move forward in our vision, energy moves towards us at that moment. It opens up the next action, the next door, the next opportunity.

Any integration tips:
Use your object as a means of inspiration and remembrance. Wear it or put it on your altar and connect to it daily.

When we take a leap of faith, new territory opens up that we did not see before, and we gain access to information not previously available. When we risk believing in ourselves, we will be amazed at the support that comes. We will recognize that doing this work is what we were born to do. When we remember life not lived fully is not the life we want, then we choose.

And we choose powerfully not to turn back again. We may fail. We may fall. We may even disgrace ourselves. But what if we didn't? Or what if we did? Go forward now and live the life you were born to live! You belong to life and life belongs to you.

Sistership Circle inspires, empowers and trains women to lead women's circles. As part of our Facilitator Tribe Membership, we create monthly circle outlines. This ritual was co-created by Tanya Lynn and other advanced facilitators. http://sistershipcircle.com/become-a-facilitator

Journal Prompts: Connect to Your Purpose

What is your #1 takeaway from ritual?

What did you receive?

If you were to lead this in a women's circle, how would you make this your own?

Self Love Ritual

A Vow to Yourself

Intention and outcome of the ritual: to dedicate yourself to self-love

Introduction to Self Love Ritual:
On our path towards embracing all that we are, self love is of vital importance. It nourishes our dreams, fuels our passions and brings sustenance to our souls. Through conscious dedication and practice, we can gift ourselves the necessary appreciation, celebration and love that we deserve. This ritual is a dedication of self love to ourselves.

As with all practices and sacred workings, go with the supplies that resonate with you. Feel free to change the wording in the vows or any of the items in the ritual to suit your needs and honor the call of your intuition. Be open to how this wants to unfold for you.

Step by step instructions:
Place the candle, bowl of water, feather, bowl of Earth and token on a table or altar. Add crystals, flowers or statues if you are called to use them in your practice.

Before your sacred rite, take a moment to cleanse the ritual area with some sacred smoke or visualize a white light sweeping away any unwanted energy. Take a few deep grounding breaths and feel Presence returning as you center yourself back in the body.

Light the candle on the altar and say: "As I ignite this fire, I ignite within me the spark of divine love for myself and for my whole being. May the flames of self love burn ever brighter with each passing day keeping me warm, setting fire to my creative flame and fueling my desires."

Materials and supplies: rose quartz, rhodochrosite, rhodonite, pink calcite (for self-love), citrine, larimar, carnelian (for increasing esteem and self-worth), flowers to adorn altar and yourself, statues, nature items for altar, candle, small bowl of water, bowl with small amount of earth, feather, token, ring or talisman to gift yourself

> May the love I hold for myself take flight, soaring ever higher in the skies.

Place a hand on the Earth and say: "Gaia, as I connect to your soil, I connect to my own roots digging them deeply into my truth and into self love. As I walk upon your Earth, may I be grounded in a place of knowing my worthiness, my dreams, my desires and the depths of my own body. May I embody wholeness, wellness and harmony. May I honor the needs of my body."

Take a sip of the water and say: "As I drink deep the waters of the world, I drink deep of my own wisdom, intuition and guidance. May I trust the whispers of my inner knowing and read carefully all that is written on the walls of my heart."

Pick up the feather and say: "May the love I hold for myself take flight, soaring ever higher in the skies. May I be open to my dreams, my goals, my feelings and the gifts that I bring into this world. As I will it, so it is."

Make this vow to yourself:

"I (name) vow to love myself with every fiber of my being. To be here to listen with an open ear when my intuition has words of wisdom for me, to honor and care for this temple and to walk the path of my deepest truth. I pledge to be the heroine of my journey, follow the call of my desires, ask myself for what I need, and honor what it is that I want to do. I promise to dedicate energy to balancing my wellness and to supporting

Any integration tips:

You can continue to tap into self love and nourish your intention on a daily basis with affirmations such as the following.

I love and accept myself unconditionally
I radiate self love
I fully respect myself
I honor my intuition and follow my inner compass
I am worthy of unconditional love from myself and others
I love myself more every day
I acknowledge my gifts and the medicine that I bring into this world
I am worthy of my needs, desires, and goals
My feelings, thoughts and desires are important and valid

Adapt the affirmations or add some that resonate with you. When you are finished your ritual, celebrate yourself. Dance, sing, drum or have a sacred fire in honor of your re-you-nion with yourself.

my wellbeing. I pledge to embody this Earthly form and take up space, speak my truth and never put myself on the shelf again. I, (name) commit myself to me from this day until the end of my days. In deepest dedication to myself and my heart, as I will it, so it is. Blessed be."

You can give yourself a token in honor of your pledge, a ring or talisman to seal your dedication to yourself and keep with you as a reminder of your self love vow.

When you are finished, thank the spirits or Universe for being present for your sacred rite. You can release the dirt, water and any flower petals you wish to give back to the Earth outside in sacred offering.

Gratitude Gift

Be ready to make magic with the New and Full Moons!

Want to create powerful Lunar rituals and manifest big changes, love or abundance? Download this FREE Moon Practices eBook here by Ara of The Goddess Circle

https://thegoddesscircle.net/offerings/moon-medicine

C. Ara Campbell is a visionary writer, author, priestess, and founder of The Goddess Circle. She is a soul guide, cosmic channel, facilitator of *The Inner Priestess Awakening Online Journey* and *Relationship Empowerment & Sacred Love Online Journey*, and author of *The Astro Forecast Publication*. She is the bestselling author of *Dark Goddess Magick* and contributing author on the books *Journeys with the Divine Feminine* and *Original Resistance: Reclaiming Lilith, Reclaiming Ourselves*. Ara is a modern day mystic dedicated to empowering others and connecting them with their purpose, living embodied truth and healing using the natural world. Ara is an old soul that has been writing and channeling guidance from the unseen since she was young intuitively soul coaching using spiritual and natural energies. She can often be found seeking wisdom and solace in the wilds of Mother Earth, capturing the magic of nature with her camera or snuggling her dog Sonny. Learn more at: https://thegoddesscircle.net/

Journal Prompts: Self Love Ritual

What is your #1 takeaway from ritual?

What did you receive?

If you were to lead this in a women's circle, how would you make this your own?

10,000 Mirrors

Partner Eye Gazing Ceremony

Intention and outcome of the ritual: to experience the world/partner as a mirror of the self

Introduction to 10,000 Mirrors:
This is a partnered eye gazing meditation. The partners pick each other. They sit across from each other with a lit candle in between them. If there is a dining room table, you can fit 4 couples at each corner. This is a long meditation, so make sure if people are sitting on the floor they are comfortable! In back jacks or lots of pillows behind their backs. This meditation is done at night and lasts about 45 minutes.

Take your time. You don't need too many verbal cues. Leave long silences between cues. Less is more. The participants will be allowing the journey to unfold. This meditation will do the work for you.

Many may have never done eye gazing before and this can be a very vulnerable connection to themselves. They will be experiencing their partner morphing into different faces and different identities. These faces are all from their perspective, with the idea that the world is our mirror, so what they see is what is inside of them.

Step by step instructions:
Instruct partners to begin off facing each other with the candle in the middle, eyes closed, and sync their breaths together, breathing into their bellies and grounding together.

Materials and supplies: candle

Have them begin breathing into their hearts. Alternatively, you can have them use the "trance dance" breath: 2 sharp inhales through the nose and one strong breath out the mouth to over oxygenate the brain and induce trance. Use whichever method you think is right for your circle.

Once you feel the room is in sync, ask them to now open their eyes and begin to lock eyes, either beginning with the right eye or the left eye first. They look at each other right eye to right eye or left eye to left eye. Right eye is usually the easiest to start with for most people, especially beginners. Let them know they can close their eyes whenever they need to, if it gets to be too much.

Then they begin to sync their breaths. The hard part is done now, you have created the space and the circuit. Now let the journey unfold. Remember, you don't have to say too much!

You can use simple verbal cues like:
What do you see in the sacred mirror?
What is unfolding before you? Alternatively: Allow your mirror to unfold before you.
How far can you surrender?
Let your eyes get soft.
Go deeper into the eyes.

Half way through the meditation have them switch eyes.

The key to the 10,000 mirrors meditation is to really focus on the surrender, letting their eyes get soft, and staying present.

Once they have done both eyes and about 45 minutes has passed, bring them back, having them just softly

The key to the 10,000 mirrors meditation is to really focus on the surrender, letting their eyes get soft, and staying present.

close their eyes and come back into their own bodies, acknowledging this outer journey of the inner realms. Place their hands at their hearts, open their eyes and bow to each other.

Open for journal time and silence time.

Any integration tips: If this is used during the weekend retreat you can do it right before bed and just keep it silent until the morning time. It's important to allow for an integration as deep as this work.

Gratitude Gift

Receive inspiration, stories, and a good dose of badass medicine.

https://www.globalturnon.com/newsletter-sign-up

LeahRose Farber is a powerful mentor for women in leading other women - complete with a web of support, the confidence to lead, and a way to bring their powerful magic to the world. She is the founder of the Worldwide Women's Circle, an international movement that brings women leaders together all over the world in synchronous women's circles. Her international training program, Sacred Badassery, empowers women all over the world to become women's leaders in their own right. LeahRose is a Master Healer, Shamanic Priestess and Wild Woman. She is also a practical business woman and wife. Learn more at: http://globalturnon.com

Journal Prompts: 10,000 Mirrors

What is your #1 takeaway from ritual?

What did you receive?

If you were to lead this in a women's circle, how would you make this your own?

Clear, Bless, and Protect

A Sacred Smudging Ceremony

Intention and outcome of the ritual: to provide protection and grounding through sacred smoke

Introduction to Clear, Bless, and Protect:
The burning of sacred plants is an ancient ritual widely used in many cultures. The specific practice of "smudging" comes from Indigenous Peoples in North America, who have long used this ritual in their sacred ceremonies. We give thanks to them and Mother Earth for the blessings of this ritual.

To perform smudging in your circle, first prepare the materials in advance, which can be bought from local or online spiritual supply stores. Please purchase from a supplier that supports ethically and sustainably sourced sacred plants. For safety and spiritual purposes, it is best to perform this ritual outdoors. If you must perform it indoors, ensure the windows are open so that the smoke can escape and be cleared from the room.

Step by step instructions:
Ensure all materials are placed on the circle altar. Share some insight and your intention for why you are smudging with fellow sisters (to clear everyone's energy, get grounded, protect the circle, whatever feels right).

Materials and supplies: abalone shell, 1 or more sacred smudging plants (white sage, cedar, sweetgrass, juniper, lavender sage, rosemary, matches, smudging feather (optional)

Ask all sisters to stand up in a circle. Choose the sister to your left to be the first to be smudged. Ask her to spread her arms out like eagle wings, and to set an intention for the ceremony, such as "I now release everything I need to for my highest good."

Ask all sisters watching to open their hands and bring them to their hearts, palms facing outwards towards the sister receiving the smudging. Ask all sisters to beam white, pink, or golden light of love, healing and protection from their hearts and hands to the sister being smudged. Ask them to send her a heart prayer, such as, "May our sister release all she needs to for her highest good." As fellow sisters beam out love, face the recipient sister and bow in love and reverence to each other.

Burn the sacred plant in your shell and waft its smoke using your hand or a smudging feather over the sister, beginning at her heart. Move up towards her head, and waft all around the outline of her body in a clockwise direction. Ask her to lift one foot at a time and smudge beneath her feet. When you finish smudging her front side and feet, walk behind her and smudge her back side, top to bottom. Come back to her front and end at her heart. The entire process of smudging a sister should take just a couple of minutes.

> As fellow sisters beam out love, face the recipient sister and bow in love and reverence to each other.

Bow to each other in love and gratitude to complete her smudging. Pass the smudge shell to her, and invite her to smudge the sister to her left, and the next sister to the one to her left, and so on. You will be the last sister to receive a smudging from the sister on your right (although it's best to smudge yourself and your space before sisters arrive/when preparing the circle).

Close the ritual by asking everyone to sit in circle and place the tools back on your altar (put out the burning plants) as you offer thanks to the sacred elements, the sacred lands and the sacred circle. Offer up any other prayers of protection and grounding. You are now all energetically cleared and protected, and feeling loved and connected. May all sisters and your sacred circle be blessed with magic and miracles as you continue your circle.

After the circle, surrender the cooled ashes of the smudged plants to Mother Earth with a final prayer, so that She may transmute the energy of all that was released for everyone's highest good. Blessed be!

Gratitude Gift

Goddess Meditation

Embrace your Sacred Feminine gifts of abundance, love, pleasure, power, joy, radiance, compassion, intuition, clarity, wisdom and more with Syma's beautifully guided Goddess initiation meditation and chakra activation journey.

http://flourishinggoddess.com/freegoddessmeditation

Syma Kharal is an international sacred feminine and spiritual coach, healer, speaker, retreat leader and #1 Amazon bestselling author of "Goddess Reclaimed" and "Manifest Soulmate Love." She is dedicated to empowering soulful women heal their deepest wounds, manifest their boldest dreams and flourish in every way, into the Goddesses they are. Learn more at: http://FlourishingGoddess.com

Journal Prompts: Clear, Bless, and Protect

What is your #1 takeaway from ritual?

What did you receive?

If you were to lead this in a women's circle, how would you make this your own?

Old Bones

Giving Your Old Stories to the Fire

Intention and outcome of the ritual: to release and give to the fire that which is no longer true

Introduction to Old Bones:
Living is about consistently dying and shedding that which no longer supports life. That is what happens in the Fall, when the leaves drop and the grass dries. There is a rightful and needed time to drop, surrender and truly let something go or die. This ritual is to help with letting go of an old story that no longer supports you. The story can be a mental story that you tell yourself that isn't true or helpful in your evolution, like "I am not enough because_____" or " I will never amount to anything because _____." The story can also be an actual event that happened in your life, an occasion, a moment that you no longer want to relive or share with others in the same way. As Joseph Campbell said, "The familiar life horizons has been outgrown; the old concepts, ideals, and emotional patterns no longer fit; the time for the passing of a threshold is at hand."

This ritual was gracefully given to me by my friend Brie, who often lives connected intimately to nature, off the grid in the rugged mountains of Big Sur California, alongside a river with her partner Brendan. They share a sweet and creative life, living simply, gardening often, tending to animals, and are expecting their first child this Spring. I deeply respect their choices and ways in which they honor life and each other. I lead women's camping retreats on their little pocket of nature every Spring and Fall and this ritual has become one of the rituals we share.

Step by step instructions:
Have every woman grab a stick in nature to bring with them to circle around the fire. Have the women start thinking about a story or a thought whose time has come to let go of.

Materials and supplies: found sticks, a bonfire

Gather with your sisters around a bonfire outside in nature, ideally somewhere private where you are safe to talk and share intimate things. Start circle with a song or a prayer or with some slow smooth breathing. Center yourself and connect as a group.

While holding the stick you brought to the fire, take turns sharing out loud a story, idea, or thought that you tell yourself that you are ready to no longer share or energize. Be real with yourself that this story ends here, this will be the last time that you share this story in this way. Make sure it is a story that has grown old and no longer serves you, a story you maybe have been carrying around with you for awhile but now it's time has come for you to let it go. Make a pact with yourself that this is the moment with these women as witness that this story is over.

Share your story out loud while looking right at the fire. Don't look at others, tell the story to the fire. All the witnessing women are to look at the fire as well, not at the women speaking. Share as much as the story as you are ready to let go of. Take your time as you talk, breathe, feel and share from your heart. Once you feel complete, say out loud "This story is no longer mine," "I now let go of this story," or "I give this story to the fire," which ever way feels authentic and brings you closure.

Sweep your stick over your body to clean your bones. Sweep the stick down both arms and legs and anywhere on your body that needs help in releasing the story. Break the stick, if possible, and give that stick and the story that is now in it to the fire.

Repeat with the women who are also ready to share and let go. Thank the fire for taking your old stories and transforming them. End with a song or a prayer or an offering to the fire.

> Make a pact with yourself that this is the moment with these women as witness that this story is over.

Tawny Sterios is a mother, a yoga teacher and teacher trainer, a doula, circle guide and nature enthusiast. She has been teaching yoga for 15 years and leading women's circles and retreats for the last 10 years. A RYT-500hr yoga teacher, co-founder of mBODY Yoga a studio she owned for 8 years in San Luis Obispo CA. She is certified in both Kundalini Yoga and LEVITYoga, and is a certified Pre/Post Partum Doula and a Pre/Post Natal Yoga Instructor. Tawny teaches yoga lifestyle principles in LEVITYoga's Teacher Training Programs, and has been leading monthly New Moon Women's Circle at studios near and far for a decade. Leading Spring and Fall women only camping retreats in Big Sur CA is her latest fun creation. She takes a group of yogis to India every February as a part of a group retreat with Sevanti Adventures. She was a featured model in Yoga Journal Magazine (2010-2011) and was one of a select group of national instructors invited to teach yoga at the White House for Michelle Obama's anti-obesity initiative (2011-2013). Tawny's passion for life and warm presence makes her teaching style very approachable and accessible to students of all levels. Learn more at: http://tawnysterios.com

Journal Prompts: Old Bones

What is your #1 takeaway from ritual?

What did you receive?

If you were to lead this in a women's circle, how would you make this your own?

The Wise Woman Inside of You

Seeking Inner Guidance

Intention and outcome of the ritual: to listen for the wisdom of your inner Wise Woman

Introduction to The Wise Woman Inside of You:

This ritual is designed to help women get specific answers and advice from their Higher Self. It works well for any group of women because they will each "fill in the blanks" in terms of their own specific challenge.

Step by step instructions:

Begin by taking the women through a bodily relaxation exercise. Have them all inhale and exhale deeply and slowly together, with eyes closed. Then guide them verbally, starting at their toes and soles of their feet, to "release, relax, let go" of each muscle group or body area, moving up from their feet to ankles, calves, knees and so on. Especially have them release their lower jaw when you get to their heads. Once you have thoroughly taken them through a full body relaxation, end this part by saying, "Now you find yourself right behind your eyes."

Begin the actual journey by inviting them to picture themselves in a beautiful place in nature. It can be someplace they have already been or simply a place they would like to go, perhaps by a body of water, a forest, or a mountain. It is someplace they love being and they feel very safe there.

> Invite the women to ask their Wise Woman for advice or guidance about an area in life where they are challenged right now.

They see a path up ahead and decide to follow it. The path leads to a gate to a walled-in garden. They open the gate and continue to follow the path. Looking ahead, they see their Wise Woman sitting on a bench, waiting to greet them. They give their Wise Woman a hug, feeling her loving gaze upon them. She beckons them to sit down next to her on the bench.

Invite the women to ask their Wise Woman for advice or guidance about an area in life where they are challenged right now. After waiting a few moments, instruct them to listen carefully as their Wise Woman answers their question. Give them at least 3 or 4 minutes here, then guide them out of the garden, back to the gate, and back to the path leading to the beautiful place in nature.

Speak louder and quicker as you tell them to feel the energy and balance coming back into their bodies, quickly taking them from feet to head with energy and power now. Have them gently open their eyes when they are ready.

Snow Thorner has created, led and participated in hundreds of circles in Canada, Afrika and the U.S. Snow has trained with, participated and led authentic feminine leadership programs with the Sistership Circle since 2014. With the caring heart of a life coach, Snow has a special calling to create a safe, warm and comfortable space for women of different races, ages, beliefs & backgrounds. She graduated from the prestigious Coaches Training Institute (CTI) in 2002. Snow is also an adept Quantum Facilitator. Snow shares her life with her beloved John Rudolph. They divide their time between a gingerbread house near Ashland, Oregon and their part time retreat center, Peaceful Valley Hideaway ranch in Yreka, California.

Journal Prompts: The Wise Woman Inside of You

What is your #1 takeaway from ritual?

What did you receive?

If you were to lead this in a women's circle, how would you make this your own?

Creating the Space of Sisterhood

Archetypal Invocation

Intention and outcome of the ritual: to invoke and invite the archetypes within to circle space

Introduction to Creating the Space of Sisterhood: This is a space creation ceremony piece to help evoke the energies of the female archetypal energies.

Step by step instructions: Read this as the opening of the circle:

I light the candle for the maiden within us all. She laughs and dances. She sheds her clothes and rolls down hills. Full of joyful energy and curiosity, she playfully pushes past boundaries and breaks down walls with her laughter. I send out the call to bring forth this energy into this circle. Be here now.

I light the candle for the mother within us all. She who nurtures. She, the caretaker. She, who sets necessary boundaries, even if the boundaries exist solely to be pushed against. The mother holds out her open arms and allows us to find comfort against her breast. I send out the call to bring forth this energy into this circle. Be here now.

I light the candle for the crone within us all. Wise woman, full to the brim of life experiences. She who understands the meaning of grief and also understands truest joy. She who has let go the trappings of societal shame, to blossom fully into the woman of all knowing. I send out the call to bring forth this energy into this circle. Be here now.

I light the candle for the warrioress within us all. She who instinctively protects. She loves fiercely, and fights with all of her heart. Passion drives her in everything she pursues. She who is single minded and stubbornly defends what is hers. I send out the call to bring forth this energy into this circle. Be here now.

I light the candle for the goddess within us all. She who pulls the tides and sees all cycles. She who holds a space of unconditional compassion and she who guides us through the hardship to a place of perfect clarity. I send out the call to bring this energy into this circle. Be here now.

I light the candle for our grandmothers across the veil. They hold the wisdom of generations, of hard work, sacrifice and mistakes made. Lessons learned reveal clarity. I send out the call to bring this energy into this circle. Be here now.

I light this candle to hold this space with the intent of [connection or circle intent]. This is our space. We are here now.

Ivy Rose Latchford is a wife, Wiccan high priestess, ritualist, devotee to Aphrodite and a fur momma to two adorable fur-babies. Growing up with a love of nature and the earth, it was natural that, after a long and twisty path, Ivy came to walk alongside the divine feminine. She believes that the goddess lives in each of us, and aligning ourselves with our inner goddess leads to happiness and abundance. She is the high priestess of Twilight Spiral Coven in Orange County, and the creatrix of the Rising Fire Tribe group on Facebook. She also leads Red Tent ceremonies and teaches classes and workshops in the Orange County area. She has many 1:1 and group programs available. Learn more at: http://ivyroselatchford.com

Journal Prompts: Creating the Space of Sisterhood

What is your #1 takeaway from ritual?

What did you receive?

If you were to lead this in a women's circle, how would you make this your own?

Your True Self

Being Who You Are

Intention and outcome of the ritual: to gain fresh clarity on who you are and what you desire

Introduction to Your True Self: Clarity is one of the primary pillars in Sistership Circle. It is easy to get bogged down in "how" to do something, and that worry can create confusion. Getting back to a place of clarity reconnects you to your "why" and is a clear place from which to lead.

Step by step instructions:

Exercise for the Self:
Fold the piece of paper in half like a book, then turn it to landscape orientation and place it in front of you. With whatever pen you choose, write your first name as large as you can across the paper.

Materials and supplies: a piece of paper, pens, a piece of food that you love

Think of all the roles and identities you have: relationships, families, faith or religion, gender, ethnicity, job title, degrees, everything you can think of. Write all of these things down on the same side of the paper, wherever they will fit. Maybe some of them overlap your own name. Take as much time as you need to fill up that paper with every aspect of who you are in the world.

When you're finished, take some time to gaze at the paper. Read the words written down. Consider that even the name you wrote down first, your name, is a label that was given to you. Can you see your Self still there, under all those roles you have? Perhaps you've become a little buried, a little submerged under all these identities, and therefore have lost some of the clarity of who you are.

Notice, however, that everything you see on that page is on the outside: the outside of the page and therefore, symbolically, on the outside of you. This is how other people see you, how other people approach you: as their sister, mother, colleague, friend.

Now open the piece of paper. Look at the clear space, how there's nothing visible there.

The inside of you is vast, much much bigger than the outside. You are full of infinite possibilities, and clarity is possible from this blank space.

Ritual:

Take the piece of food you brought, something that you desire, something that you love. When you love something, when you desire it deeply, you should embrace that desire. Put away all distractions and focus on what is in front of you. Right now, put all of your intention on this piece of food. Savor it. Fulfill your desire for this food. Focus on how it feels to hold in your hand, to put into your mouth. Pay deep attention to what it tastes like and how it makes you feel. Allow everything else to fall away and allow this desire to be fulfilled.

Any integration tips: How can the experience of fulfilling your desire for a food inform how you fulfill what else you desire for your life? What do you learn when you drop into that vast emptiness within yourself?

Tara Nedbalek-Mayne & Lara Kasza co-created and led this ritual for the How to Lead Circle level 1 Certification program.

Tara Nedbalek-Mayne is a coach, healer, teacher, Level 2 Sistership Circle facilitator, and fierce advocate for the truth. As Tara processed through the rewriting of her stories, and embraced her healing, she began to witness the ripple effect the healing can create. As a painter, she's been learning ways to incorporate the healing vibration of art therapy into her coaching.

Lara Kasza is the creator of SandStory Therapy® and a Creative Psychotherapist using the medium of sand and symbols. She works with amazing Therapists and Counsellors seeking a safe space for personal development. She has a beautiful and spacious SandStory Centre in North West London [Stanmore] where she also offers Training, Supervision and Coaching in SandStory Therapy®, SandStory Skills®, SandStory Supervision® and run SandStory Circle® groups. Learn more: https://www.larakasza.com/sandstory-therapy

Journal Prompts: Your True Self

What is your #1 takeaway from ritual?

What did you receive?

If you were to lead this in a women's circle, how would you make this your own?

Weaving Community

What Does It Mean to Belong?

Intention and outcome of the ritual: to tune into the essence of belonging and community

Introduction to Weaving Community: Each of us is an individual within one or more communities. Sometimes it can be difficult to figure out how and who we are in those communities. Anchoring ourselves in sisterhood and weaving our community together helps bring us back to the core of belonging.

Step by step instructions:

Visualization:

Pick up your bundle of sticks or pens. If you don't have any physically, imagine that you are holding some. Hold the bundle in one hand. This is you and a community. As you hold that bundle of you and your community, what energy do you get from that? What are you sensing? What are you feeling from holding your community in your hands?

Materials and supplies: bundle of sticks or pens, beads, thread or string

Now take one stick or pen out of the middle. This is you. You're an individual that belongs to that community. What emotions does that evoke? In any way you like, hard or soft, fast or slow, throw all the sticks away except for the one that is you.

How do you feel, as that one person? Have you experienced this separation now or before in your life? And if you had been supported, or if you had asked for support, would that have changed your experience and how you felt?

Ritual:

Gather your beads and string. If you happen to have a bead that's bigger or brighter than all the others, pick up that bead first. If they're all the same, pick up one that's calling to you. Put your

string through this first bead and and bring it all the way down to the end of the string, holding it so it doesn't fall off the other end. On the long side of the string, tie a knot above the bead, big enough so that the bead can't slide back down the string. This bead is your goddess bead, the one that anchors and unites you with your sisters.

Continue to thread beads and tie knots as you invoke energies and give gratitudes in the following way:

Thread a bead, tie a knot. Say aloud: I invoke the energy of _____, which I have received from our sistership community and will pass on to other women as I spread my wings and soar as a feminine leader.

Thread a bead, tie a knot. Say aloud: I invoke the energy of _____, which I send to each of you for those times you are in need.

Each bead represents a true sense of belonging within yourself and within your community of sisters. May you always feel the presence of your sisters supporting you. When you are complete, bring the two ends of the string together and tie a final knot, joining the thread into a circle.

This ritual can be done by yourself or in circle. If you are on your own, simply continue threading, tying, and invoking. If you are in circle, each woman may speak aloud her invocations as each sister threads and ties their beads, moving around the circle until each woman is complete.

Possible energies to invoke include: vulnerability, confidence, support, gratitude, love, authenticity, intuition, friendship, compassion, hope, faith, the wise woman, presence, freedom, belonging, surrender, inclusion, courage, acceptance, community, clarity, magic, truth

Any integration tips: Place your beaded circle on your altar, use it during meditation, or wear it throughout your day. Use it in any way that connects you to belonging and sisterhood.

Nicki Simonich & Katrina Young co-created and led this ritual for the How to Lead Circle level 1 Certification program.

Nicki Simonich is an intuitive, conscious space holder, who mindfully guides her clients through the layers of healing to live a more empowered, authentic life. As a Certified Integrative Life Coach and a Trauma Informed Yoga Therapy and Meditation teacher, Nicki specializes in PTSD, anxiety, chronic pain, chronic stress, and life transitions. She is a compassionate, kind, and wise healer who is always ready to meet you exactly where you are. Learn more: www.MindBodyTruth.com

Katrina Joy Young is the founder of Dragonfly Alchemy. Dragonfly = Change, transformation, self-realization, Joy, Ancient Wisdom. Alchemy = changing from one form to another. Creating the life you want to live. From pain to freedom. She has mastered awareness of the body from 15 years of practicing and teaching Pilates and a lifetime of studying modalities such as reiki, bowen, medical intuition, spirituality, and Women's Circles. katrina@dragonflyalchemy.com.au

Journal Prompts: Weaving Community

What is your #1 takeaway from ritual?

What did you receive?

If you were to lead this in a women's circle, how would you make this your own?

Feeling Your Intuition

Self-Empowerment Declaration

Intention and outcome of the ritual: To reconnect to the feminine wisdom and confidence within you

Introduction to Feeling Your Intuition: To connect with your confidence and intention is to invoke the divine wisdom that is your inner authority. As you connect with your inner authority and confidence, you make space for your most authentic self to rise and unveil the divine goddess within.

Step by step instructions:

Meditation:

Materials and supplies: Frankincense oil, Citrine crystal, Candle (to stitch in)

This meditation is a "yes or no" technique designed to help you connect to your inner authority, your intuition, for decision making. Your intuition is the communication you receive in your body from the higher dimensional part of you, the all knowing part of you, which most people call their higher selves, or inner authority. This is the part of you that connects to your soul or source. It connects the dots between the part of you that's an individual and the part of you that contains all the knowledge of the universe. Having this intermediary is immensely helpful in building your confidence, because you can ask an exact question--yes or no– and receive the answer in your body.

Begin by sitting comfortably and taking a deep breath in, feeling your nose and abdomen expand on the inhale and contract on the exhale. Continuing to breathe and soften, access a memory that gave you great joy in that moment. For some people, this is a great vacation. For others, it's a family reunion. Maybe it's the sound of a child's laughter or a hug from someone you love dearly. Put yourself back into that time and space and allow your body to feel the way it did then. Feel the sensations running through you and where and how you feel them in your body, especially in your chest: do your shoulders and lungs expand? Do you feel lighter? This is the feeling of Yes.

Return now to the present moment, continuing to breathe into your belly. Notice how your chest feels in this neutral state.

Now think of a memory that brings you great pain or sorrow, when someone may have trespassed against you, said unkind words, or hurt you deeply. Place yourself into that situation just long enough to feel the shift in your body, especially noticing how your chest area changes: does your chest contract and feel heavier? Do your shoulders round? You may even feel a strong density in the middle of your chest. This is what a No feels like.

Return again to the present moment, releasing all of the previous feelings with a deep cleansing breath.

Now you know what it feels like when your higher self answers your questions. Sometimes you get a yes, sometimes you get a no, and sometimes the answer will be neutral. In order to get the most accurate and useful answer from your higher self, it can be useful to use a template for your question: Higher Self, is it beneficial for me to do _____ at this time? Remember, the higher self is all knowing, in that you need to be very specific when you ask the question.

Sometimes, you might begin to feel the answer before they're even done asking the question. That lightning speed usually means it's an immediate Yes. If you get a strong Yes, you can proceed without hesitation. If you receive a no or a neutral response, it might be beneficial to walk away, either entirely or to recalibrate. Occasionally, you might feel a slight yes. This answer indicates that there's either a more complex question or there may be more factors that need to be worked out.

Ritual:

Frankincense oil clears away the self judgment that blocks you from fully owning and trusting your inner authority and claiming your self empowerment. Begin by applying a drop of Frankincense to your throat, abdomen, and forehead.

At a deeper level, the secret to confidence is your self-esteem, your inherent self worth. You can think of self-esteem as the state of being and your confidence as the act of doing. When a woman is centered and connected to her core, she is connected to her self-authority and claims self-empowerment as her birthright.

Make your self empowerment declaration with sacred intention. Place your hand on you heart and read the following statements out loud:

> Today I stand in my full embodied sovereign will as a creatrix.
>
> I stand in my highest truth, self love, power, and authentic voice in this lifetime.
>
> I choose my best and highest timeline to fulfill my soul's mission.
>
> I intend for this to be the highest good of all.
>
> In gratitude and honor of my ancestral line and each and all of my karmic relations, I will do my full authority as a divine being of light.
>
> I call my full power and energies back to me now.
>
> I forgive myself and all those who disempowered, dishonored, and disconnected from me from my highest truth with words, intentions, or actions.
>
> I stand in my sovereign power and authority over my life.
>
> Unhealthy bonds, patterns, and painful karmic ties that have influenced me, consciously or unconsciously, are broken and cut now.
>
> I now extract and call to me only the wisdom pertinent to my current lifetime, from all past lifetimes, free from all drama, trauma, and karma.
>
> I cut old trauma, or unhealthy attachments to any future generations.
>
> These patterns and their effects end with my declaration here and now.
>
> I nullify, cancel, erase, delete, clear, disentangle, and remove all negative, discordant energies from my subtle energy fields, chakras, auric field, all bodies, and Akashic records.
>
> These are now released from all timelines, spaces, dimensions, parallel universes, and past, present and future lifetimes: not only of my own, but of my ancestors and my descendants as well.
>
> The past is clear and clean.
>
> I am a sovereign divine being.
>
> I seal and sanctify this decree with the sacred love and light of the Divine.
>
> So be it.
>
> And so it is.

Any integration tips:

How can we each walk away feeling more confident?

What do you need to boost your confidence?

What are your unique gifts that you bring as a leader?

Ronnie Dearlove & **Stephanie Kalson** co-created and led this ritual for the How to Lead Circle level 1 Certification program.

Ronnie Lee, Mother and Grandmother, has facilitated spiritual gatherings, workshops and development circles since 2006. Holds many traditional qualifications – JP(Qualified), Minister, B.S.Sc, Dip Justice, Dip Child Development, Dip Child Psychology, and many metaphysical qualifications – Teacher of Essence of Angels, Crystal Light Healing, and Aetheric Healing, Reiki Master, Seicheim Master. Her circles strengthen your connection to Mother Earth – Gaia, Father Sky – Cosmic energies with meditation, sacred geometry, oils, essences, crystals, and rituals to realign all levels of your Soul's potential via your Heart's connection to YOU.

Stephanie Kalson had a vision during Covid that she would weave a circle of women together pulling them out of isolation, help build deep connection and lifelong friendships. She believes that it is our sacred duty to step into our power, tap into our divine feminine wisdom, and lead a movement towards conscious living and fostering soul purpose. That when sisters come together in unconditional love and support with divine feminine flow, the shift we need to see and feel will ripple out, gracing our lives in abundance, joy and peace. Stephanie has over 25 years as an operations and logistics manager in corporate commodities. She is a Certified Psychiatric Technician and is currently enrolled in university for Psychology. She is a Psychic Medium, a Certified Clinical Hypnotherapist, and Transformational Teacher, seeing clients online and in her Stratford CT office.

Journal Prompts: Feeling Your Intuition

What is your #1 takeaway from ritual?

What did you receive?

If you were to lead this in a women's circle, how would you make this your own?

Swirling Snowflakes

Clearing the Vision for Your Soul's Desires

Intention and outcome of the ritual: to settle the snowflakes and connect with our inner clarity

Introduction to Swirling Snowflakes: Our minds can often be like the inside of a shaken snow globe. Swirling thoughts, stories, and busy-ness can cloud our vision, but stillness is the gateway to our soul's desire. When we get quiet, we can find clarity.

Step by step instructions:
Visualization:
Find yourself in a nice comfortable place. Close your eyes and take a deep breath in. Picture yourself sitting on a mountaintop inside the snow globe of your life. You've been here many times before. You know there is a magical expansive vista all around you. But your vision is blurred by all the snow: the noise, the chaos, and the busy-ness swirling around you. Notice all the forces that are agitating your snowflakes– thoughts, beliefs, self-talk. All the things that keep you from seeing your truth.

Materials and supplies:
a crystal for clarity

Now take a few moments to pause. Place one hand on your heart, the home of your intelligence and your wisdom. This is the place where your soul resides, the place where your unique essence lives, the birthplace of your deepest desires. Tune into this powerful, compassionate, wise, loving center and ask yourself, "What area of my life would I like to have clarity in today?"

Once you've selected an area, tune into your heart and ask yourself, "What does success in this area look like to me? What is it that I most desire in this area?" Allow whatever is there to unfold, trusting your inner knowing.

As your snow globe finds its grounding and the snowflakes begin to settle, your vision becomes clearer and clearer. Open yourself up to all possibilities, trusting that if you can see it, if you can feel it, then this is guidance from your soul. This is your soul's desire. Allow it, trust it. You begin to feel a sense of excitement and joy. As confusion becomes clarity and you see your vision unfolding and manifesting before you, tune back into your heart and soul.

Ask yourself, "What would make this vision even more successful?" You have even more clarity to see the bigger picture of what is possible for you. Allow whatever is there for you to come, knowing that you have the potential to create anything your heart and soul desires, because you are a powerful manifestor. Ask yourself again, "What else would make this vision more successful for me?" Drop back into your heart and offer thanks and gratitude for the whispers you have received from your soul. The snowglobe acts like a crystal ball to your soul, revealing words, wisdom, and guidance from your innate knowing. Give thanks to the essence and the beauty of you that has been expressed in your vision.

Ritual:

Hold your chosen crystal where it feels potent for you. Read the following poem out loud:

> "Today I Choose Myself" by Shiloh Sophia McCloud
> I choose to be the queen of my own domain.
> To name myself as the one who governs my life.
> I shall not wait for the approval of others
> in order to act on my own behalf and inner knowing's.

I choose to listen to this great heart within me.
To honor what it wants, needs, and longs for.
I shall no longer allow the sacred parts of myself
to be fragmented and isolated and hidden.
I choose to take up space in this universe and it's call.
To inhabit and uplift this vessel of self, which is my temple.
I shall not keep my gifts to myself any longer
or allow my fear to keep me from my greatness.
I choose to be as wonderful as I truly am.
To explore just who I might be, after all these years.
I shall not judge myself for where I have not
journeyed, yet, or the ways I have been untrue.
I choose to forgive myself and any of the old stories.
To make space for new stories, legends even, to emerge.
I shall not forsake my dreamings and visionings or allow
others ideas to crowd my own. I will think my own thoughts.
I choose to fall in love with who I am, as I am, today.
To embrace the messy and the marvelous in me.
I shall not diminish my light, one day longer.
I am releasing the shadows, right this very moment.
I choose to see you, and to be seen by you, too.
To find and dance with those who are ready to choose.
I choose to see myself as whole, holy, worthy,
so much more than enough. I choose to be glorious.
Being glorious is not the default. It is a choice.
And today, I choose myself.

Any integration tips:
What are the snowflakes that swirl in your head? How can you find stillness and allow these snowflakes to fall?

Cindy Scott
& Carla Bonner
co-created and led this ritual for the How to Lead Circle level 1 Certification program.

Journal Prompts: Swirling Snowflakes

What is your #1 takeaway from ritual?

What did you receive?

If you were to lead this in a women's circle, how would you make this your own?

Inner Jewels

Breaking The Box

Intention and outcome of the ritual: to break the box that keeps your gifts locked inside

Introduction to Inner Jewels: The brilliant gifts you are here to share with the world are already within you. It is your birthright to let them shine bright. Yet, often there is something that seems to stand in the way. When you break through what blocks you, you can bring your gifts into the world fully.

Step by step instructions:

The Cave of Jewels Meditation:

Bring your awareness to your heart beating in your chest. Here, in the heart space, is where past hurts live. Disappointments and vulnerabilities reside here, and so too does joy and passion. Bring your awareness even deeper into yourself, into your soul. Through the pain and the passion is a deep layer, a dark cave, a place beyond anything that has affected you.

Here is where we find our raw instincts. Here at our core lies the truth. It is the foundation that supports us and holds the building blocks of authenticity. Down deep within your core, a candle lies dormant. Pick that candle

Materials and supplies: a paper box, markers

up. Feel its weight in your hand. What color is it? However you choose, light the candle wick. When you do so, you will see a cave full of jewels come into view, sparkling in the light of your candle. These jewels reflect the deep worth that is hidden in your recesses. Observe the Sapphire of Self-Love, the Pearls of Wisdom, the Gems of Joy. Watch the light glimmer and dance on the jewels and precious metals.

These are your superpowers, your expansive wealth within. This is you.

Bring your attention back into your heart space, now filled with the light radiating from the cave of jewels. Your heart chakra is filled with heat and power. Feel the value and worth you've found. This is your natural state, and with ease and joy, you can return to this feeling of expansive riches anytime.

> The brilliant gifts you are here to share with the world are already within you.

Ritual:

What are the thoughts and feelings that prevent you from sharing your jewels with the world? What stands in the way? Take up your box and markers. Write every fear, judgment, doubt, and block you can think of onto the box. Anything that stops you from showing up in the world as the radiant powerful person you are in the cave of jewels. Be beautifully, painfully honest as you write.

When you finish, take a few minutes to observe this box deeply. Look at its size and shape and the things you've written onto it. Each written thought is a wall, a boundary, a limit between you and embodying the jewels that you know are within you.

Now, begin to tear the box apart, smash it, break it. Piece by piece, claim your power. What's available on the other side are treasures and abundance, the core of who you are.

Any integration tips: What color was your candle in the cave of jewels? What jewels shone the brightest? What do you know about your worth now that you've broken through the box?

Dulce Mendoza, Dani Hill, and Maria Chowdhury co-created and led this ritual for the How to Lead Circle level 1 Certification program.

Dulce Mendoza lives in Fresno CA and enjoys the outdoors, especially the beach. She is a loving mother to a joyful daughter and a wife to a blunt and hardworking husband. Her vision is to create a space for women to gather and experience the freedom to be authentic, playful, and creative. She is learning to say YES to my heart and with an open heart, and says YES to Sistership Circle where women can feel safe to BE.

Dani Hill has two kids, two dogs, a bird, a tortoise, a bunny, three fish, two tenrecs and a wife. She runs her own business working with kids and you will find Dani at the park hugging trees when she is not cooking and caring for my family. Circle work has opened doors for Dani, allowing and encouraging her to use her crystals, essential oils and meditation practises to enrich the lives of women in her community. Growing up in rural Victoria, Australia and then coming to Las Vegas, Nevada in her early 20's allows Dani to have a unique perspective on many aspects of life.

Maria Chowdhury has twenty years of experience as a home birth midwife, herbalist, meditator, and Qigong practitioner, which has prepared her to hold potent medicine and sacred space. Currently, she midwifes spiritual women in the midst of powerful life transitions and supports them to navigate the trail ahead to stay aligned with their essence and connect to their power even in times of uncertainty and confusion. As a temple guide, she holds sacred space for the extraordinary and arduous experience of birth and transformation to unfold safely and organically. Learn more at www.pathwithharmony.com

Journal Prompts: Inner Jewels

What is your #1 takeaway from ritual?

What did you receive?

If you were to lead this in a women's circle, how would you make this your own?

Confidence and Competence

The Inner Wisdom of Knowing Enough

Intention and outcome of the ritual: to connect with your intuition and worthiness and access your confidence within

Introduction to Confidence and Competence: The core of confidence is self-esteem: not that you know everything, but that you know enough to be in flow. Confidence is knowing that you are competent. Your intuition, inner wisdom, and internal authority are the true sources of confidence.

Step by step instructions:

Materials and supplies: a piece of clay (in a color that speaks to you)

Guided Visualization:

Imagine yourself outside in nature, walking down a path. It's bright out: look around. What do you see? What is the environment like? What kind of vegetation is around? Take a deep breath in What does the air smell like? What do you hear? Take a moment to tune into your senses.

Keep walking down the path. It's starting to get dark. Just as you're starting to wonder if you should keep going, an animal appears and begins to walk beside you. After a few steps, the animal steps forward and begins walking in front of you. You have the feeling that it wants you to follow, so you do. After a while, the animal turns and looks right at you. Feel its calm presence and its steady gaze. As you continue to follow the animal, you come to a clearing. The animal stops and sits in the middle of the clearing. In front of them is a large rock that looks like it would make a good seat.

Feeling the animal inviting you to join it, you sit down on the rock. As you do, you notice something on the ground. It is a gift from the animal. Pick it up and look at it, then hold it to your heart. Take a moment to look at the animal, then gaze deeply into its eyes. It has a message for you. Open yourself to receive the message in whatever form it comes.

Ritual:

Notice the love you feel for yourself, which is the unconditional love you feel for others. Breathe into the willingness of finding your inner peace. Truly forgiving and liberating from suffering. Inhale, feeling the knowingness in your heart. You are here, you are present. Let the sense of relaxation melt away any tension that may arise in your body. Be present at this moment and begin to feel grateful to have eyes to see, ears to hear, hands to touch, a heart to feel.

Breathe deep into the sense of gratitude. Allow your heart to radiate in appreciation to be alive. Our heart is at the center point of our physical bodies, and the midpoint between our beloved Mother Earth and Father Sky, our connection to the spiritual plane. Feel the unconditional love of Mother Earth and Father Sky. Take a deep breath in, put the palms of your hands to your heart, and inhale this unconditional love, happiness, compassion, and oneness of the universe.

With your eyes closed, look into your mind's eye, your third eye, the all seeing eye. Breathe deeply, finding an alignment from your heart to your third eye. They work together as a divine partnership to access your true inner soul, your higher self. Welcome your higher self and see your inner true being. Once you do, you are relaxed and truly free. You are powerful, loving, and wise. You are calm, light, and relaxed. With your palms still against your heart, connect now to who you are. What do you wish to ask the universe? Do you have a prayer in your heart?

Connect with your inner wisdom and hear the message that is there for you. With complete trust, extend your hand and allow the universe to respond with a gift. Notice the shape of your gift. Notice the weight on your hands and allow the answers to your prayer to come through this gift.

Give gratitude to the universe for the gifts that are in the making and for the gifts that have been received. Breathe into your heart, feeling the warmth of your breath igniting the fire within. Your passion and love illuminate your inner being and radiate out into the world. You are whole and complete, perfect as you are.

With your eyes closed, reach out and take hold of your clay. Continue to feel that sense of gratitude and confidence, worthiness and love. Let that be your guide to molding your clay. Connect with your higher being. Trust your intuition. Allow your intuition to guide your hands.

Let the message that is coming through for you be an expression in your creation.

> **Give gratitude to the universe for the gifts that are in the making and for the gifts that have been received.**

Any integration tips:
What message did you receive from the animal that came to you in the visualization? What does the new shape of your clay reveal to you?

Dulce Mendoza and Chloe Hemsworth co-created and led this ritual for the How to Lead Circle level 1 Certification program.

Journal Prompts: Confidence and Competence

What is your #1 takeaway from ritual?

What did you receive?

If you were to lead this in a women's circle, how would you make this your own?

The Manifestation Diamond

Releasing to Receive

Intention and outcome of the ritual: to build stronger connections with our hearts desires and heal the sister wound

Materials and supplies: bowl of water, pen, paper

Introduction to The Manifestation Diamond: Women's relationships in mainstream media and literature are usually portrayed as toxic and competitive. We have been conditioned to believe that we must constantly be in competition with other women, to be jealous of what a sister has, or to turn against our sisters in order to maintain our power and status in this patriarchal society. We have all experienced this sister wound in some way throughout our lifetimes. Many of us can recall the wounding that's happened to us, as well as times we have wounded another sister. We heal these wounds by reinforcing our boundaries and shifting our focus from competition to connection and collaboration.

Step by step instructions:

Water Cleansing Ceremony:
Sit in a comfortable position and place the bowl of water in front of you. Place one hand on your heart and one hand on your belly. Close your eyes, breathing deeply, and call in the divine guidance you feel most connected to at this time.

Ask them to be here with you now, to assist you in gently, peacefully releasing the cords and hooks that no longer serve your highest good.

> We heal these wounds by reinforcing our boundaries and shifting our focus...

They are with you now, surrounding you and protecting you with a circle of bright, golden, shimmering light. Feel their presence and love surrounding you. With gratitude in your heart, say to yourself:

"For what once was, I release, I forgive, I heal. I let go of any attachments to places, people, situations, thoughts, feelings, or ways of being. I ask that all cords attached to me that are not aligned with love, light, and positive attention be released gently and peacefully. Help me to release them and surround me with a healing light to protect me from future attachments. Thank you."

Slowly open your eyes and softly focus your gaze on the bowl of water before you. Place your hands over the water. Imagine that you can see the healing light that continues to surround you flow down through your crown chakra, into your heart chakra, and out through the palms of your hands into the water. The light that flows from your palms energizes the water with pure light and love. The light you send forth into the water blesses the water and transforms it into healing water, vibrating with the energy of universal and unconditional love.

Slowly and reverently begin to wash your hands in the bowl of water, repeating this affirmation out loud:

"Let this water wash away all the resentment, hurt, and trauma that no longer serves me. I forgive those sisters who knowingly or unknowingly hurt me in the past and I set them and myself free. Their actions will no longer determine my destiny. I forgive myself for knowingly or unknowingly hurting another sister and I wash away any shame I have been holding. I am free. Sisterhood, love, and support is my new reality. And so it is."

Dry your hands and set the water aside.

Ritual:

On a sheet of paper, write down any blocks you wish to remove in order to step into your higher power. These could be situations or events in the past, or people who have wounded you. Get it all out, then set this piece of paper aside.

On another sheet of paper, draw a big diamond. Begin at the top point of the diamond, at the North, which is connected to fire, our passion, confidence, and truth, our Sacral Chakra. At this North point, write what is physically true for you right now. Once it is written, you are physically grounded in the now. You are present and here.

Move to the East point on your diamond. The East is connected to air, the throat chakra, your true desire for what you want in your life. At this point, write down what you want, as if it is already done, as if it is already yours.

Move to the South point on the diamond. The South is connected to water, to healing growth, intuition, feeling, and the heart chakra. So far you have been grounded and put your wishes out into the universe. Now, how does it feel you're living your true dharma? Your desire has come to be. How does it feel?

Finish in the West point on the diamond. The West is connected to the earth and is grounding, solidifying, powerful, and connected to your root chakra. Put yourself in the physical feeling and sensation of experiencing your true heart's desire.

Release it to the universe. Say here is my desire, my wish. I'm ready for it to come into my life.

The last step in the diamond manifestation, once you've written everything down, is to let it go.

Release it to the universe. Say here is my desire, my wish. I'm ready for it to come into my life.

Trust that the universe has received it and it is on its way.

Remember to hold your vision and the feelings. Create space physically and energetically for your manifestation to enter, knowing in your heart that it is done and will happen.

Keep your diamond in a safe place, somewhere sacred and special to you. Bring it out for a new moon to reenergize your manifestations and to resolidify your desire. On a full moon, create the energetic and physical space for it to come into your life by taking the piece of paper on which you wrote all that's blocking you and destroying it.

Any integration tips:
Keep your diamond in a safe place, somewhere sacred and special to you. Bring it out for a new moon to reenergize your manifestations and to resolidify your desire. On a full moon, create the energetic and physical space for it to come into your life by taking the piece of paper on which you wrote all that's blocking you and destroying it.

Dani Toews and Julia LoPresti co-created and led this ritual for the How to Lead Circle level 1 Certification program.

Journal Prompts: The Manifestation Diamond

What is your #1 takeaway from ritual?

What did you receive?

If you were to lead this in a women's circle, how would you make this your own?

Money Stories

What You're (Self)Worth

Intention and outcome of the ritual: To gain clarity around the relationship between money and self-worth

Introduction to Money Stories: Often we struggle with the idea of charging for our services, and those challenges often come from our money stories. Sometimes in healing work, there are stories about offering your services for money, whether it be that you "shouldn't" charge for them or that those services are only available to people who can pay for them. Your money story might be tied into relationships or family. Usually, your money stories are wrapped up in your sense of self-worth.

Step by step instructions:

Guided Visualization:

Let's journey to a time when life was simple and people were more connected to the earth and to each other. Envision a small rural village surrounded by a forest dotted with little cottages. One of those cottages is your new home. Enter your cottage and take a look around. What is it that you see? How is it furnished? Is there artwork on the walls? Take a moment to enjoy your new space. Curious about your community, you step outside and walk the path into the village. It's early morning and the vendors are setting up their carts in the marketplace. The shopkeepers are just opening up their doors. You pass by the carts, looking at their wares. There's a cart with luscious fruits and vegetables. You see a cart with handcrafted jewelry. You see beautiful fabrics and pottery. Suddenly, something catches your eye in one of the store windows, like sunlight glinting off a shiny object. It calls to you and you walk over. When you first step in front of the window, all you see is your reflection. As you step closer, your reflection fades, and you see the most exquisite vessel you have ever seen.

Materials and supplies: a bottle or pitcher filled with water and a sacred glass

What does this vessel look like? What is it made of? Is it glass? Is it pottery? Is it wood? What color is it? Is it shiny? Does it sparkle? When you look at it, you are filled with awe. You must know more about it, so you enter the shop to speak to the shopkeeper

A beautiful, wizened woman greets you. She smiles radiantly. She knows why you have come. She takes the vessel from the window and places it on the counter. "This elixir is the most powerful of all," she says. "It supports your authentic self and elevates your vibration to bring you in alignment with your purpose. Its ingredients include confidence, courage, connection, compassion, love, empowerment and worthiness. It is the elixir of the Priestess, the Wise Woman, the Mother and the Queen." You ask the woman, "How much does this elixir cost?" The woman smiles again. She says, "Sister, the question is not how much does it cost. The question is, what is it worth to you?" She takes out a slip of paper and hands you a quill pen. She asks you to write down on the paper what this elixir is worth to you.

You feel connected, connected to the women, connected to source, connected to the community, and more connected to yourself...

See yourself writing on that slip of paper what it is worth to you to receive and become all that you desire, to truly take ownership of the ingredients in this elixir.

You fold the paper three times and hand it back to the woman. She drops the paper into the vessel and it magically disappears into the elixir. "It is yours," she says as she hands you the vessel. "However, for the elixir to have its full effect, you must follow these instructions:

In the middle of the marketplace, there is a pool of water. Long long ago that pool had a fountain which produced a never ending flow of water. However, one day the fountains cease to flow. The pool still collects water from the rain but it is not nearly enough to serve our village. You must go to this pool, sit in the middle, and drink your elixir. You must give gratitude to the source, to the ancients, to the guides for all that you have received. This is all that is asked of you."

You agree to follow the instructions and you leave the shop feeling excited and joyful. You walk directly through the center of the market and find a round pool about ten feet in diameter. You lift up your skirts and put your feet into the water. It is warm from the sun and comes just above your ankle. You walk to the center and sit. You close your eyes. You whisper words of gratitude and then you drink the elixir. You feel it pass over your lips and fill your mouth, trickle down your throat and fill your body. You feel a warm glow expanding inside of you. The elixir fills you with a wonderful bubbly, sparkly effervescence.

Instinctively, you raise the empty vessel above your head, and suddenly, water begins to pour out of the vessel. It cascades in a beautiful waterfall all around you.

You notice that several other women have come to the fountain, each carrying their own vessel. They stand around the pool, and as the water flows from your vessel, these women stretch out their arms and catch it in their own vessels. They give thanks and gratitude for all that they have received. When the water stops flowing, the women ask you, "How can we repay you for all you have given us?"

You answer: "What is it worth to you?"

You head back to your cottage for the evening, giving thanks and being grateful for all that you've received. When you awake the next day, your vessel is full again. Hugging it to you, you make your way once more to the pool. When you arrive, the women are waiting. Each woman has brought an item to honor you and to honor the gifts you have shared with them. One has a small bag of gold. One has a beautiful bracelet she made especially for you. One has a loaf of freshly baked bread. Another has a beautiful basket she's woven. You thank the women and take your place in the center of the fountain. And once again the water begins to flow. The women fill up their vessels, and then they too lift their vessels over their heads. Water pours from their vessels, which in turn fills the vessels of more women who are blessed by what they have received.

As you walk the path back to your cottage, you feel humbled. You feel full and yet light. You feel connected, connected to the women, connected to source, connected to the community, and more connected to yourself than ever before. You place your vessel on the window sill in the moonlight. You climb into bed and lay your head to rest. Deep within you, you know this is your purpose. You are all that you were meant to be. And you now know without a doubt that you are worthy of such gifts. You are worthy.

> **Any integration tips**:
> Journal: What are three things that you possess that give value or that are value or worth to your circle? What is one money block or limiting belief that prevents you from moving forward?

Put your hand on your heart and the other on your solar plexus..

This is the center of your personal power. Feel your self-worth.

Ritual:

Take up your pitcher or bottle of water and your empty glass. Imagine that the pitcher or the bottle of water is your beautiful vessel full of the elixir. Pour some of the liquid into your glass. Hold up your glass and say the following affirmations out loud:

> I am a sacred vessel.
>
> I am full of infinite possibilities.
>
> I am infinite.
>
> I am worthy of the gifts I have received.
>
> I am worthy of being honored for sharing my gifts.
>
> I am blessed with abundance.
>
> I give thanks and gratitude for all of my blessings.

Drink the elixir.

Michelle Merlo and Kristin Walcott co-created and led this ritual for the How to Lead Circle level 1 Certification program.

Journal Prompts: Money Stories

What is your #1 takeaway from ritual?

What did you receive?

If you were to lead this in a women's circle, how would you make this your own?

Belonging in Sisterhood

The Gift of Vision

Intention and outcome of the ritual: to connect deeply with ourselves and our sisters

Introduction to Belonging in Sisterhood: One of our basic needs is a feeling of being connected. We are all social animals and women especially thrive when they have a sense of belonging and community. Through sisterhood, women are able to make deep and lasting emotional connections.

Materials and supplies: a comfortable seat, a circle of 2+ women

Step by step instructions:

Grounding Meditation:
Begin to call your authentic parts and pieces into your heart center: your emotional system, mental system, physical system, and spiritual system. Say to yourself, "I am centered." Bring your focus from your heart center up through the top of your head, to a source of pure light that flows directly into you. Allow this light to travel down through your head, through your heart, and into your womb space. Find a still point in the center of your womb space. Feel the light fill you as it travels

down your legs and out of the bottoms of your feet, into the Earth, to a sacred space that belongs only to your energetic system. Say to yourself, "I am grounded."

Envision a shield of protection surrounding you, as though you are the filament at the center of a light bulb. The light bulb itself acts as a container and a boundary for your energy. And just like with a light bulb, when your light is flowing, the light not only fills up the light bulb but radiates beyond the bulb. Say to yourself, "I am contained and have boundaries."

See that light flowing from your heart, up through source, back through your body and heart and back down into that sacred space in the center of the earth before flowing back up through your legs and filling your light bulb with light. Say to yourself, "I am filled and flowing."

Place your right hand over your womb space. Breathe into that still point in your womb space and say to yourself, "I am a creator."

> **Any integration tips**: How can you integrate all that you are? How is each sister a reflection of every other sister's brilliance?

Place your left hand on your heart. Find that still point in your heart center. Say to yourself, "I am love."

Bring your right hand up to the center of your forehead and place two fingers over the still point in the center of your brain, between the pineal gland and the pituitary gland. Say to yourself, "I am still."

Ritual:

Create a space where women have a chance to give the gift of vision and receive the gift of being seen. Going around the circle, one woman will receive while each of her sisters shares the gift of their vision for her, their wishes for her, their reflections of her magnificence.

Suzanne Chenoweth and Marnae Hobson co-created and led this ritual for the How to Lead Circle level 1 Certification program.

Journal Prompts: Belonging in Sisterhood

What is your #1 takeaway from ritual?

What did you receive?

If you were to lead this in a women's circle, how would you make this your own?

Meeting Your Guides

Connect with Your Spiritual Team

Intention and outcome of the ritual: to connect with your spirit team

Introduction to Meeting Your Guides: Community and belonging are deeply rooted needs, but for many women they can also be wounds. Connecting with your spirit guides is a valuable tool to remind you that, regardless of where you are or with whom, you always have support and guidance.

Step by step instructions:

Meeting Your Guides:

Through this meditation, you will connect with guides that you will invite to be on your spiritual team, into your community, to be here for you whenever you need them.

Materials and supplies: music to help you journey

Put on the music that will help you on your inner journey. Come into a comfortable position and begin to slow your breathing.

In your mind's eye, visualize your heart. As you connect with your heart space.

As you visualize and connect your heart you see a door. The door opens and a beautiful deep light pulls you in. You land in a garden full of healing trees. As you begin to walk forward, feel Mother Earth beneath your feet. Allow the music to guide you. In front of you is a rushing waterfall. You sit beneath it and allow it to wash away anything that doesn't serve you anymore.

Feel the cooling water wash over you, cleansing and purifying.

When you're ready, walk back to the garden. Place your hands on your heart and send an invitation to your spirit team, your guides: angels, gods, goddesses, teachers, ancestors. Invite them to be part of your community. They belong with you and you belong with them. With your team, you're never alone. You have them in your energetic field, you can visualize them, connect with them, call upon them anytime you need support.

Take some time to ask questions here in this beautiful space. Ask your guides what message they have for you today. Allow their messages to flow, their guidance and wisdom. Know that you can do this at any point simply by placing your hands on your heart and directing a question to your guides. Ask them, and trust that they will guide you on the path that will bring you the most joy, happiness, trust, and wisdom.

In your mind's eye, visualize your heart. As you connect with your heart space.

Any integration tips:
Identify a time and space where you felt like you belonged, and a time and space where you felt like you didn't. Who are your guides? What messages do they have for you?

Zuleimy Jaimes and Annette Bizzell co-created and led this ritual for the How to Lead Circle level 1 Certification program.

Journal Prompts: Meeting Your Guides

What is your #1 takeaway from ritual?

What did you receive?

If you were to lead this in a women's circle, how would you make this your own?

Invoking the Elements

Gain Clarity on Your Why

Intention and outcome of the ritual: to get clear on or reconnect with your Why for leading circle

Introduction to Invoking the Elements:
Your Why is your motivation for leading circle. Discovering your desires and your passions, your joy, what truly makes you feel alive, all of these things lead to your Why. Getting clear on these things can help you see what your purposes are and what is true for you.

Step by step instructions:

Visualization:

In a comfortable seat, close your eyes and breathe deeply, in and out, at least 3 times.

Materials and supplies: a heavy candle, quartz and/or hematite, lemon essential oil, a glass or chalice of water

Imagine that you are arriving at a circle gathering. It can be a circle that you've been to before or somewhere new. You could be outdoors in nature or inside. Anywhere you imagine is perfect. Notice your surroundings as you approach the circle. What does the space look like?

As you move closer to the circle, you hear quiet, warm, and inviting voices. You can begin to see some of the other women sitting in the circle. There may be some familiar faces or some new and exciting ones. Some of the women smile at you as you come closer.

Notice how you feel as you come up to the circle, seeing the women move aside and make space for you to settle in. Perhaps they place a hand on your shoulder warmly or invite you in for a hug. Notice how many others are sitting there in circle with you. Notice if there are any altars or sacred ceremony spaces around. As you sit down, notice if it's a soft pillow you're sitting upon or if there are blankets on the ground. Notice if there is a scent of incense lingering in the air or if you can hear any soft music or outside noises around you.

Once you settle in, look around you at all the beautiful women. They are gazing back at you with love and compassion. Look into their eyes and into their hearts. Feel the safety and sacredness of the space and the circle. This is your sanctuary, your community. These are your sisters and they are here for you. Continue to imagine yourself in deep connection with your circle. Notice what you are feeling and experiencing. Allow yourself to be fully immersed in this sacred circle.

Now look up from where you are sitting. You are drawn to a woman across from you. She appears older. Perhaps she's the crone of the circle. As you lock eyes with her, you can see the deep pools of wisdom inside her eyes. You realize you are connecting with the Wise Woman. You can feel your intuition awaken as she stares deep within your eyes, into your soul.

You hear her Sage voice inside your mind as clear as a bell. She asks you, "What is it that you desire here?" Allow yourself to receive any messages and to notice anything else from within the circle.

Feel yourself gently awakening from the Wise Woman's trance. Carry with you any messages you received, from her or from your higher self. Feel that the circle within your mind's eye has come to a close for now, and gently bring your awareness back to this time and space.

Take a few minutes and write down any messages you may have received, any desires or needs or wants that came up, or anything you discovered that you were passionate about while you were in this circle

Ritual:

Bringing in the 4 elements can help set your intention for your own circles.

Place a few drops of lemon oil in the palms of your hands. Rub your hands together and breathe in the scent. Lemon helps to clear our vision for our intention.

Repeat the following out loud: Goddess, Spirit, Universe, I give thanks to you for all the blessings in my life. With the element of Air, I cleanse any beliefs holding me back from my deepest desires for my circle, to prepare for a new beginning and for the highest good. So be it.

Inhale that clarity and exhale any limiting beliefs. Visualize them leaving with your exhale and allow your vision for your circle to become crystal clear.

Imagine a bright rainbow around you growing brighter and brighter, stronger with every breath.

Light your candle. The flame will absorb any negativity, and eliminate any fears or limiting beliefs, taking them up with the smoke of the candle. As you stare into the flame, think of anything that might be holding you back from your dreams as a circle leader. Release them into the flame.

Repeat the following out loud: Goddess, Spirit, Universe, I give thanks to you for all the blessings in my life. With the element of Fire, I release my fears and ignite my desires as I am encouraged to prepare for a new beginning and for the highest good. So be it.

> Feel the safety and sacredness of the space and the circle. This is your sanctuary, your community.

Pick up your glass of water. Allow your energy to blend with the energy of the water, giving something to the water for its life giving properties. Take a sip of the water and put down your glass.

Repeat the following out loud: Goddess, Spirit, Universe, I give thanks to you for all the blessings in my life. With the element of Water I give strength and energy to the future to prepare for a new beginning and for the highest good. So be it.

Pick up your quartz with your left hand, point facing in towards you, and your hematite with your right hand, point facing away from you. Allow the quartz to bring clarity to your desires and ground those desires with the hematite. Allow the Earth's energy to assist in manifesting your hopes, wishes, and your dreams for your circle.

Repeat the following out loud: Goddess, Spirit, Universe, I give thanks to you for all the blessings in my life. With the element of Earth I manifest my wishes to welcome in my divine feminine leadership as a circle facilitator to prepare for a new beginning and for the highest good. So be it.

To close the ritual, give thanks to the elements for their help by tapping your foot three times on the ground. Say goodbye and send them on their way.

Place your ritual elements on your altar and allow them to carry your intentions and desires.

Any integration tips:
Write a declaration for your circle. Be specific about who, what, when, where, and how much. Say it out loud and place it on your altar.

Tara Brietta is a Mind-Body Wellness Practitioner. Her journey into the Healing Arts began in 2007. She first completed a Mind-Body Wellness diploma program at the Southwest Institute for Healing Arts in Tempe, Arizona. She then returned and graduated in February, 2012 with an Associate's Degree in Mind-Body Transformation Psychology. In addition, Tara is a certified Life Coach, Hypnotherapist and Reiki Master. She also has a passion for Tarot and Oracle Cards, Astrology, Numerology, Crystal Healing and Animal Totems.

Abbegail Eason is a nurse, intuitive coach and holistic aromatherapist. She leads circle to create the experience of belonging that she was craving after living abroad for many years. She offers a compassionate, open-hearted approach that allows women to feel supported and accepted while finding their own way through hard things. She is messy, real, imperfect and she has dedicated her life to honoring the same in her clients. When she is not traveling, you will find Abbe in her current hometown of Beaufort, South Caroline soaking in the glorious natural beauty and smell of the LowCountry. Learn more at http://abbegail.com.

Journal Prompts: Invoking the Elements

What is your #1 takeaway from ritual?

What did you receive?

If you were to lead this in a women's circle, how would you make this your own?

The Anointed Goddess

The Art of Anointing in Sacred Circle

Intention and outcome of the ritual: to embody your promise with sacred oils

Introduction to The Anointed Goddess:
When I envision a Goddess, I see a woman unshackled, unapologetic, and unfretted with worry or fear; completely free to be her colorful expression of waves of wonder, of textured emotion. I see her past, present, and future clearly because there is nothing to hide; she is proud of her curves, her wrinkles, her bruises and scars for they tell her story, that which is proud. She wears her soul upon her chest, allowing the heart to magnetize each step she makes.

She is the Anointed Goddess.

Materials and supplies: a sacred oil, chosen thematically

Step by step instructions:
When gathering in sacred women's circles, it is customary to cleanse and clear the energy of the circle before, during, and after with items such as sage and or palo santo in the north, south, east, and west quadrants of the circle, including the entrance. Each Goddess that enters the room would benefit greatly from being smudged by the sage and or palo santo by placing the smudging bundle all around their aura and under their feet. This clears away the past for the Goddess so she can be fully present. A clearing mantra repeated for several minutes is highly recommended. Diffusing oils of ancient scripture such as Sandalwood, Frankincense, and Myrrh provide protection from unwanted interferences. During the circle I would encourage one or some of these items to keep the energy pure during the circle: toning with the women in song, in sound, with a welcome mantra, a 7 metal bowl, crystal bowl and tuning forks will provide clearing during the circle. I recommend ending circle with a chosen song that becomes your ritual song such as the Pagan Goddess song:

> "May the circle be open but unbroken
>
> May the peace (love) of the Goddess

Be ever in your heart

Merry meet,

And, merry part,

And merry meet again."

Once the energy is pure, it is now time to anoint the goddesses who enter with an oil of the month, the season, or for a specific medicinal intention. I recommend having an arsenal of oils in your sacred circle tote to claim each circle as its own. For example, I would encourage the aroma of Lavender to soften and calm the circle during a hectic week such as Mercury in Retrograde, heightened political controversy, astrological mayhem, etc. You as the circle leader are intuitively guided to pick the right oil because you are the pulse of the circle.

In the beginning, I often pass the bottle of anointing oil around to share the scent of the oil with the ladies to initiate the mood of the evening. It isn't until the very end of circle that we anoint.

She wears her soul upon her chest, allowing the heart to magnetize each step she makes.
She is the Anointed Goddess.

Gratitude Gift

Essential Oils 101

Incorporating pure grade therapeutic essential oils into a healing ritual experience is a sure-fire way to help aid the process along more smoothly. Scent carries with it emotional memories and can be a powerful antidote to any dis-ease. I teach about these precious oils and if you'd like to learn more, please reach out to me: TheAnointedGoddess@gmail.com

Each woman would proclaim a promise out loud to the circle before she is anointed. For example: If the theme was "Embody Your Feminine," a woman would say something like: "I embody my feminine by swaying my hips to the rhythm of my heart and crying whenever I feel like it." She would be anointed by the anointing sister of the ceremony, and the anointing sister and the entire circle would repeat back to her as she is anointed (on her hands, feet, ear lobes, and collarbone), "You embody the feminine by swaying your hips to the rhythm of your heart and crying whenever you feel like it."

Chandra Nicole McAtee, a Peace Activist, is a woman of the people fascinated by Social Psychology. Chandra's life experience holds its place in the natural world as well as the digital world--one foot on the pulse of mother nature the other on human evolution. With a Masters in Educational Technology, a Holistic Health Practitioner, Yogi Chandra wants nothing more than for women to fall madly in love with themselves. Chandra has taught Health & Wellness for many years in Public, Private, and Non-Profit schools and organizations. Chandra has studied Shamanism, Somatic Therapy, Yoga Therapy & Craniosacral Therapy--to compliment her efforts towards understanding humans and what they specifically need to feel whole and complete; ending self-hate forever.

Journal Prompts: The Anointed Goddess

What is your #1 takeaway from ritual?

What did you receive?

If you were to lead this in a women's circle, how would you make this your own?

Becoming the Seer

Unveiling Your Psychic Gifts

Intention and outcome of the ritual: to see and be seen in your mystical, multi-dimensional wholeness

Introduction to Becoming the Seer:

This activity allows each participant to become more comfortable and confident with their unique psychic gifts unveiled during this gathering with the help of the facilitator. Each participant takes a turn to see each member's essence unveiled (with their given permission) and to share what they see (their inner perception of each person's essence) out loud with everyone participating in the circle. It is a safe space where we celebrate the paranormal and metaphysical multi-dimensional aspects of our beings.

The facilitator/mentor has to be knowledgeable and experienced with intuitive guidance regarding soul reading, metaphysical inner sight styles, and diversity of spiritual/intuitive gifts.

All participants must be aware of the nature of this activity prior to joining and they must feel comfortable with the facilitator as the trust and safety elements are very important for this activity to flow and flourish organically. This activity is very intimate in nature and it is more appropriate for advanced students in the mystical path.

Step by step instructions:

The facilitator/mentor opens up the circle/group experience by setting an intention or prayer for this event, in order to prepare the sacred space and to create the energetic intention for the experience.

Depending on the facilitator/mentor's style (preferably warm and informal), the next step would be to introduce all participants to each other. Follow your intuition and feel the participants personalities and energetic makeup to decide what style of ice breaker would be best. Tailor it for each group meeting in order to tune into the present moment, their energetic essence, and feelings/moods at that specific time. When doing an informal introduction, you may have each participant introduce their name and to share briefly what is their unique experience with the multi-dimensional and metaphysical/paranormal realm. Pay attention to each participant, how they feel and present their story, as this can give you an idea of where they are at in regards to their comfort level with these subjects, so that you can also tune into how to better support their experience during this circle activity.

Once everyone is introduced, ask for a volunteer to begin the circle experience. Then, you both tune into and openly share/explore the appropriate given details regarding this person's style of inner sight so that the participant on the sharing seat becomes more aware of this gift and on how to possibly express it during this activity in order to support and encourage confidence and trust in their unique gift and own intuition.

The participant in the sharing seat then invites all other participants in the circle, one by one, to be seen by her and to hear her inner perception of their unveiled essence. The participant on the sharing seat will begin by asking for permission from the first volunteer: "Do you give me permission to unveil you and to see your soul's essence?" Once the participant to be unveiled agrees to be seen, then the participant on the sharing seat will proceed by expressing/describing how her inner sight sees the soul's essence of the receiver; she can also share feelings and sensations given by her intuitive guidance that can complement the inner sight visions.

The receiver has an opportunity to be seen in a very intuitive and sensitive way. She gets seen and she is also witnessed by others in a more multi-dimensional way. At the same time, the Seer is also witnessed as she is developing and exploring her inner sight more deeply. This event encourages both the Seer and the receiver to engage in a very intimate experience where both get to connect more intimately, unfold in a loving and metaphysical way with support from the mentor/facilitator and the other participants.

Once the Seer is done sharing with the receiver, she gives thanks for the experience and opportunity. The receiver is welcome to remain unveiled for the rest of the event while she cherishes herself in her intuitive sensitivity, in this loving and safe sacred space.

The Seer will perform this with each participant, going in a circle. Depending on how long this gathering is able to meet, you have the option to have each participant get on the Seers seat and be a receiver for each Seer (to be the seer and also be seen). You can also have separate meetings, where each meeting is designated to one participant to be the only one in the Seer's seat that time and each takes turns to be in the Seer's seat at designated meeting dates.

You can use this activity as a part of another group activity or event and you can also perform it by itself. If it is performed by itself, include an open sharing/Q&A time slot at the end so they can share their experience and feelings about the activity in an open, more organic and informal way. After the open sharing, include a closing intentional prayer to complete and integrate the energetic intention of the event.

This activity allows each participant to become more comfortable and confident with their unique psychic gifts unveiled...

Emelina Holland (Medicine Name: Moon Jaguar Sees the Dawn) I am a High Priestess of Love & Womb Keeper of Sacred Creative Manifestation. A Practical Mystic, Healer, Metaphysical Artist, Author, Educator, Singer, Mother, Sister & Wife. I am also the Founder of the Sacred Flame Sisterhood Circle, Sacred Root Dance, Creative Spirituality, The Creative Womb's Magic & Creative Motherhood Teachings. The work I do has been birthed through the many years of my own spiritual awakening, through my own personal healing, inner transformations and development. Learn more: http://emelinasart.com

Journal Prompts: Becoming the Seer

What is your #1 takeaway from ritual?

What did you receive?

If you were to lead this in a women's circle, how would you make this your own?

Invoke Your Avatar

Ignite Your Influence. Amplify Your Impact.

Intention and outcome of the ritual: be properly honored for your ideas or gifts, which is the secret key to unshakeable confidence and creating the impact you long to have in the world.

Introduction:

We are in a time of unprecedented uncertainty AND possibility. 3D institutions and structures are crumbling around us. We are rethinking how we relate to work, education, and other people. Things that seemed like they were never going to change have changed.

Unparalleled times call for unorthodox, creative leadership. And, I am one of those leaders. I have been preparing for times like this all my life (and for many lifetimes before this one.) When the Coronavirus hit, I pivoted easily because I have a rich inner life. But, it wasn't always that way!

In June 2010, life as I knew it fell apart. I literally crashed into life, and my only choice was to change, evolve, expand, and find new possibilities and ways of doing things. Everything looked great on the outside, but on the inside, I was miserable with my work and my marriage, I had a self-hating inner dialogue about my body, and I felt like I was dying inside.

In 2011, I made a Quantum Leap and left my secure corporate legal work and started supporting women entrepreneurs to use soul-driven business strategies to create prosperity without sacrificing pleasure and peace.

I was terrified of marketing and selling, my husband didn't support me in leaving corporate safety to take the risk to build this "weird" business, and I was going through the greatest inner conflict I'd ever experienced. My Inner Critic was telling me that I was Bad, Crazy, Too Much and Wrong. Yet, I did it anyways.

It seemed like a crazy move to go for it. I took the leap and honored my intuition over my intellect. What previously seemed crazy was actually the most sane choice to make.

In order to support you in creating your epic dream lie, in fulfilling your true potential, in taking these big leaps, I'm sharing one of my most powerful tools with you: Invoke Your Avatar. It will support you to summon unshakeable confidence to go after your biggest vision, your epic dream. Make the impact you were born to make without sacrificing financial success.

Step by step instructions:

How to find and create your Avatar

1. Go back to when you were a child and start to remember who you admired most? Who was super cool? Who did you want to be like? List ALL of them.
    a. Superheroes and heroines?
    b. Gods and goddesses
    c. Fictional characters
    d. Real-life legends

2. Now, write why you admired each one.
    a. What did you love about this being?
    b. What magical qualities did they have that you wished you had?
    c. What superpowers did they have that you wished you had?
    d. What did you love about what they wore?
    e. What colors did they use that really spoke to you?

3. Based on what you wrote above, describe your own Avatar
    a. Your Avatar is an amalgamation of the things you wrote in response to #2. If this is too much for you, if this is too far fetched, then simply tune into yourself and who you would be if you were the greatest version of yourself.
    b. Include clothing, color themes, super powers etc.

c. Include any other superpowers that appeal to you as well, things that may not be on your list already, but that you wish you had.
d. If you like drawing, create an image to go with the qualities; otherwise, just conjure your Avatar up in your imagination – this works just as well if not better!

How to invoke your Avatar

Every morning, soon after you wake up, bring your Avatar into your consciousness. Tune into her power. She is the mythic version of you, the greater than imagined possible version, and she can do anything.

Allow yourself to tap into the part of you that fantasizes and dreams. Conjure your avatar from this part of you.

Invoke her power to help you access your unshakeable confidence. Maybe even choose a pose that reminds you, and do it every morning, like Wonder Woman with her hands on her hips.

Feel her … she is strong, bold, and wise. She knows that no matter what it is that you are trying to create, you can create it.

The best part is that she's a part of you, and she's always there for you. She knows the answers to all your questions. She knows how to help you navigate all your difficulties. She has your back, always.

> She knows the answers to all your questions. She knows how to help you navigate all your difficulties. She has your back, always.

Feel her power permeating your being. Ask her for her guidance if you need it.

Create a ritual around connecting with her daily. What items help you to invoke her power? Do you want to carry some of them around with you during the day, or to important meetings or events during which you need to access your unshakeable confidence?

Your Avatar is there for you and she has your back, always! She's your secret weapon. You can lean into her.

Journal about how you can bring her qualities into the "real" world. What version of those super powers work on this plane of reality? What version of these superpowers do you already hold? Which ones are you developing?

Any integration tips:
As you start to bring your Avatar into the world more and more, you will start having the kind of impact you were born to have. You will become more and more magnetic to opportunities, relationships, and situations that seem to weave together in this gorgeous web of uncanny and surprising synchronicity.

Audio for this ritual: https://stream-tribal.s3.amazonaws.com/Women's+Circle+Ritual+Handbook/Invoke_Your_Avatar.mp3

Gratitude Gift
Epic Dream Accelerator

5 simple steps for ambitious women to access inner bliss & flow in less than 10 minutes a day and 10X productivity and fulfillment:

https://www.epicdreamacademy.com/

Kavita Rani Arora, Esq. is the founder of Epic Dream Academy® and she supports women in midlife to release their bottled up potential and finally show up as the Quantum version of themselves. It's time to stop keeping yourself prisoner and finally express what longs to pour out from the depths of your soul. As a Midlife Rebirth Guide and Spiritual Catalyst, Kavita has developed a proven energy-based process, the Epic Dream Method, for creating vibrant health, wealth, and soul-driven success derived from ancient Vedic wisdom, neuroscience, the Quantum Field, the Divine Feminine. Learn the path of dharma from someone who has walked it for many lifetimes.

Journal Prompts: Invoke Your Avatar

What is your #1 takeaway from ritual?

What did you receive?

If you were to lead this in a women's circle, how would you make this your own?

Moonblood

Honoring the Creative Life Force

Intention and outcome of the ritual: This simple ritual holds tremendous power and beauty for all in circle, and allows us to access our inherent worthiness and potency while strengthening the bonds of our local and global sisterhood.

Introduction:

As the beautiful wave of sacred women's circles continues to build momentum, women the world over are inspired to connect with our legacy of womb wisdom shared by our foremothers in red tents, moon lodges, and menstrual huts.

Honoring our Moontime (menstruation) as a time of power and sacred connection to Source is a potent ritual for women wishing to reclaim their body sovereignty and cultivate their own practice of empowered embodiment.

At Red Tent :: Louisville, we begin each women's circle with a sacred Moonblood ritual to honor those who are experiencing their releasing time during our gathering. (NOTE: For some, this may mean literal menstruation; for others who do not bleed due to any number of physical situations such as pregnancy, lactation, hormonal birth control, IUD, ablation, hysterectomy, etc., their experience of release may be energetic but nonetheless just as real and powerful as menstruation.)

The beet is chosen for this ritual due to the vibrant crimson juice that is released when the beet is cut, representing the Moonblood of each woman present, as well as the blood of our sisters and foremothers, connecting all women across time and space.

Materials and supplies:
Fresh beets (3-5 total)
Ceremonial bowl
Vegetable knife
Cutting board
Red ceremonial scarves
Smudging medium (palo santo, sage, essential oil mist, etc.)
Smudging fan or feather

Step by step instructions:

The ritual begins by first passing the basket of ceremonial red scarves. Each woman is invited to take a scarf to adorn herself if she is experiencing her releasing time, be that physical or energetic. Alternatively, the ritual may be offered to all women in the circle regardless of where they are in their hormonal/energetic cycle as a symbolic means of honoring the creative life-force in all women.

As the basket is passed, a designated sister slices the beets from root to tip, so that each beet produces 5-6 round pieces that are approximately ¼" thick. The beet slices are then placed into a ceremonial bowl. (NOTE: Slicing the beet prior to the circle will result in dried out beets that do not release juice during the ritual. For best results, wait to slice the beets until you are ready to begin the ritual.)

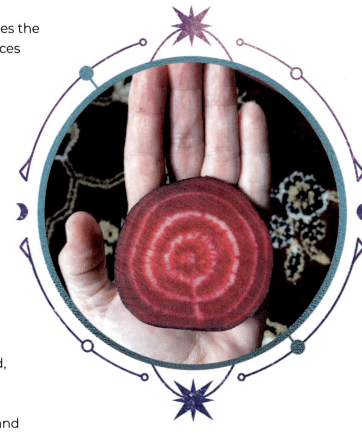

When all of the scarves have been passed and the beets have been sliced, a prayer is offered for the women in attendance as well as our global sisters with whom we are connected.

"We honor our womb wisdom and moonblood,
With reverence to our foremothers who have shared this sacred ritual,
With gratitude to the sisters who are present and love for those who are not present,
With compassion and support to the sisters who are banished to menstrual huts without the safety and sisterhood we are privileged to experience here.
Acknowledging the power of our innate ability to create and nurture life,
we reclaim our birthright to honor the beauty of our wild and wise cyclical nature.
We are reminded that our hands, which are so often used in the service of others,
may now shift to the service of our own nourishment and nurturing during this potent time of renewal.
And as we give ourselves permission to prioritize this practice of self-care and empowered embodiment, we invite our sisters, our mothers, and our daughters to do the same.
We raise the vibration of the Sacred Feminine here in this space,

And beyond this space.
To all women and all girls, everywhere.
And so it is."

After the blessing, all of the sisters in circle begin to sing Circle of Women by Nalini Blossom (which can be found here: https://www.youtube.com/watch?v=RkYshTVe1HU&t=24s), thus indicating the beginning of the ritual.

The Moonblood ritual begins with a designated sister (we'll call her the Ritualist) sitting in front of the first woman who has chosen a ceremonial scarf and offering her a smudging with sage, palo santo, essential oil or another medium of the sisterhood's choosing. The sister is then offered beet stain for her hands, applied first to one hand and then the other. The Ritualist then holds both of the cycling woman's hands in her own and offers a bow of honor and recognition of her sister's power and womb wisdom. She then moves around the circle in a clockwise direction and repeats this ritual with each woman who is adorned with a scarf while the women in circle continue to sing. When the Ritualist has offered the Moonblood ritual to all women who wished to receive it, she returns to her place in circle, and the song comes to a close.

Gratitude Gift

My offer to you is a guided meditation from my book, Wild & Wise: Sacred Feminine Meditations for Women's Circles and Personal Awakening, featuring Artemis, the goddess of authenticity.

https://redtentlouisville.com/artemis.html

Amy Bammel Wilding is the author of "Wild & Wise: Sacred Feminine Meditations for Women's Circles & Personal Awakening", and the founder of Red Tent Louisville, a sacred interfaith women's community. Devoted to inspiring and midwifing the rebirth of the Sacred Feminine from the individual to the global level, she has been leading women's circles, mother-daughter circles, and rite-of-passage ceremonies for over a decade. Amy has been featured in numerous conferences and publications including National Geographic and NPR for her work with girls and women.

Journal Prompts: Moonblood

What is your #1 takeaway from ritual?

What did you receive?

If you were to lead this in a women's circle, how would you make this your own?

Collective Invocation

Prayer for Power and Blessings

Intention and outcome of the ritual: Peace

Introduction:

The Story

In 2016, myself and a colleague brought together a group of close to 200 women in Bali for the first annual Awakened Woman Convergence. During the seven days together, we dropped the masks and facades, grew closer, and many of us walked away with women whom we would continue to develop deep sisterhoods with.

On one of the final days, our feature speaker Eve Ensler gave a rousing and passionate performance and speech. It ended with us all standing together triumphantly declaring '1 Billion Rising' - which is the slogan for Eve's organization 1 Billion Rising. Her organization is all about galvanizing one billion people around the world to rise up against violence against women. On the final notes of her speech, a crack of thunder rang through the air, as if Mama Bali was approving of this prayer. Bali is known as being one of the primary sacred power centres on the planet, with a large number of ley lines converging.

A few months later, the largest women's march would take place concurrently in close to 100 cities around the world.

> ... we dropped the masks and facades, grew closer, and many of us walked away with women whom we would continue to develop deep sisterhoods...

In 2017, we brought close to 200 people together for the second Awakened Woman Convergence, this time in Phoenix, Arizona. Known as another sacred spot on the planet for it's convergence of ley lines, our primary theme for invocation was on Awakening the Shakti.

During our Awakened Sexuality Day, we brought everyone together to focus on sexual healing. Our speakers spoke to healing the shame of sexual abuse, the power and sacredness of the womb and yoni, and how to fully release shame, fear, anger and guilt about our sexual power from our bodies.

Unexpectedly, it was also very clear in listening to the energy of the group that we needed to hold a sacred circle to heal the wounds of leadership, power, sexuality, expression and vulnerability.

As we all circled together in a radiating circle around a crystal skull, each person in the outer circles held their hand against the hearts of the person in front of them. As the host, I was called to share my fears, mistakes, vulnerabilities, and literally reveal everything I has been hiding out of fear. Being seen as 'the leader' of the gathering, it was frankly the most terrifying moment I've ever experienced and one of the most liberating. I was being asked by great Spirit to model Awakened Leadership, in laying down the masks of perfection in lieu of being witnessed in my human frailty, fragility, and authenticity.

As we went around the circle sharing our prayers into the circle, many people echoed, "I want leaders who apologize for their actions and mistakes, I want leaders who are allowed to make mistakes, I want the abuse of women and children to stop, I want to be free to express my sensuality without fear of being abused".

These prayers and words slipped from lips as the tears fell from our eyes, and we were blessed by the presence of internationally renowned singer Deya Dova in leading us in a spontaneous and unplanned tribal singing and dancing ceremony at the end.

It was only 3 days later after re-emerging onto social media again I would find out that the #metoo movement went viral on the same day as our Awakened Sexuality day and healing circle ceremony.

While these synchronicities can be discounted as being just synchronicities, there has been incredible science that has emerged over the last 30 years supporting Unified Field Theory.

For example, a large scale experiment using group mediation was done by the Transcendental Meditation organization in the late 70's in Washington, DC. The results showed a decrease in crime rates.

In 1974, an experimental study observed three different gatherings of over 7,000 people meditating each morning and evening for three consecutive weeks. The study took place in Fairfield, Iowa (December 17, 1983 – January 6, 1984), The Hague, Holland (December 21, 1984 – January 13, 1985) and Washington, DC (July 1 – July 10, 1985). The results were astounding. According to the Rand Corporation, a think-tank based in California, "acts of global terrorism resulting in fatalities and injuries were reduced by 72%." Time series analysis was used in this study to rule out possibilities that the reduction in global terrorism was caused by pre-existing trends, drifts in data or cycles.

Scientists believe this is due to a coherent resonance being created in the Unified Quantum Field by those meditating.

The "Maharishi Effect", has had over 600 scientific studies conducted in 33 countries and in over 250 independent research institutions. The evidence overwhelmingly correlates synchronized group prayer and meditation having extremely positive social, political and economic benefits to the world.

Step by Step Instructions:

This ritual can be done with any number of people, large or small. However, what determines the results is the intention and focus of the group, and the strength of embodied emotional energy.

The more focused the group is on the outcome they are wishing to see or envision, the more powerful the results will be.

You are literally and collectively envisioning a new story together with your group.

1. **Decide the collective intention:** What is the collective intention for the group? You can decide on bringing peace to a certain part of the world, prosperity for your group, or healing for a community. What will help is looking at this experience from a microcosmic to macrocosmic perspective - how are you seeking to embody and experience this personally (and why) and on a larger scale.

    For example: Your group decides to set their intentions for bring peace to Syria. How can you envision feeling peace within you and your life first and expanding that feeling.

    Using maps, visuals, and embodied emotions or stories is a beautiful way of creating more lived focus for your group.

2. **Set sacred space:** Through the use of blessing, acknowledgment and protection – set your sacred space. If online, calling in support from ancestors, guides, and the elements will help support in setting sacred space.

    Felt safety in the container also greatly supports the groups ability to relax and truly drop into your collective

---

Tips:
Seeing the work/visions as being done, already existing.

Feel the energy and invite the other participants to also feel where energy wants to move in the group. If online, allow this to happen through people sharing 'popcorn style': whoever feels called to go next, goes.

Allow spirit to work through the group in expected and unexpected ways. You may be surprised by what happens when you allow for spirit to move through the group. Often major breakthroughs will happen, unexpected weather occurrences, or even the coincidence of major world events aligning with the timing of your event. In a similar ceremony filming a ritual during the Standing Rock Standoff, the wind unexpectedly picked up right in time for our invocation!

experience. This can best be done through the sharing of real and authentic feelings devoid of competition, comparison, or jealousy.

3. **Set space for a sharing ritual:** Allow each participant to honestly and authentically share what is coming up for them in the beginning and why they are desiring to participate in this collective experience.

4. **Embodiment & Visualization:** Allow each participant to add their own prayer to the circle. If in a larger group with time constraints, allow each person to add a word or image to the group experience.

5. **Gratitude & Celebration:** Acknowledge the experience as a success and express appreciation and gratitude in thanking participants and setting the intention, "And so it is".

Gratitude Gift

Set prayers and powerful intentions in this slowly sensuous exploration of your body, breath, and pleasure with my special Sensual Liberation Temple Arts Bundle. Through soulful intention setting, building of sensual energy through breath, self-massage ritual, and other resources for the liberation of your pleasure – you'll be kneeling at the beauty of your body and praying in the altar of your body's safety, pleasure and kundalini.

https://www.phoenixamara.com/temple-arts-resource-bundle/

Phoenix Muranetz is a Sensuality Priestess, Unification Architect, and Metaphysical Guide here to support the awakening and awakened leaders in expanding their power, message and embodiment. She has landed coverage in global outlets including the Huffington Post, The Globe & Mail, Financial Post, Go TV, ShawTV, DailyHive and AZFamily TV and has spoken at events across North America. Awakened Woman has brought together thousands of people on and offline for powerful community experiences.

Journal Prompts: Collective Invocation

What is your #1 takeaway from ritual?

What did you receive?

If you were to lead this in a women's circle, how would you make this your own?

Divinely Gifted

Discover and Activate Your Divine Gifts

Introduction to Divinely Gifted:

This is a mediation with journaling prompts. Have them sit comfortably for meditation and journaling as they will shift back and forth between tuning in and writing. Make sure there is enough light to write, but not too bright for meditation.

You can play soft music if you like. Take your time with the process; it should take 45 minutes to an hour. Don't rush but keep it moving, giving a couple of minutes for each journal prompt to be written down.

Intention and outcome of ritual: To connect with the soul to reveal your divine gifts and how to best use them.

Materials: Journal and something to write with and some music.

Step by step instructions:

Instruct the women to sit comfortably with their journals and close their eyes and focus on deepening their breath. Have them put one hand on their heart.

Once they are settled and connected to their breath, start the meditation.

Instruct them to breathe in and out through your heart for the next three breaths.

Next, invite your mind and heart to come together. Let your mind slide right down into the center of your chest... like your mind is sliding down a beautiful golden slide

Let the following questions drop into the stillness of your heart, and watch where the ripples lead.

right into the center of your heart. Breathe through your heart and connect with the wisdom of your heart and soul. Wait until you feel the energy deepen and then move on to the soul questions.

Tell them: Let the following questions drop into the stillness of your heart, and watch where the ripples lead. Let the question land in your heart and trust the first thing that comes up. Then write down your answer...what came up for you. Don't censor yourself, or judge. Once you have written your answer, then close your eyes and tune right back into your heart.

Give just a minute or two to write down their answers for each question then quickly bring them back to their heart in between each question. Stay very present to hold the energy of depth and clarity.

What do you do in your own fabulous way, that's natural for you, and that you love to do?

If money were not an issue, what would you naturally do, all day long?

What do people compliment you for?

Why do people seek you out?

What do you geek out about so much that you want to know everything about it?

Tell them: You now have a list of your greatest gifts and talents! Now, rate each item on your list

Any Integration tips:
Put on some more lively music to shift the energy into action and have them walk around the room and share with as many women as possible one of their gifts and the inspired action she will take. The woman listening to the share will be as present as possible and say "thank you" then share one of her gifts and her inspired action.

from 1 to 5, with 1 being your most unique gifts. Then, circle the five highest-scoring items on your list.

Tune them back into their hearts. You will guide them through this question for each of the five gifts and have them write down an inspired action for each gift to ground it in and put it to work for them.

Let this question drop into your heart: What is one inspired action I can take to use this high-value gift?

When you go home put each action on your calendar, and do it, without question, even if it doesn't immediately make sense to you it came from your soul and your soul knows the way.

Gratitude Gift

Sacred Wealth Code Archetype Quiz

Discover your wealth creating superpower! https://bit.ly/SWCQUIZ

Prema Lee Gurreri - Vedic Astrologer | Business Oracle

Using the ancient science of Vedic Astrology and her gift of intuition Prema guides conscious women visionaries and entrepreneurs to activate their divine gifts and align with their Sacred Wealth Code, to create businesses that are aligned with their purpose. She is committed to teaching visionary women to be empowered from the inside out to live according to their soul blueprint: on purpose, in a way that is aligned with their high-value gifts and their birthright of true wealth.

Prema is the creator and the multi Award Winning author of Your Sacred Wealth Code: Unlock Your Soul Blueprint for Purpose & Prosperity, Oracle Card Deck and Journal.

https://soulutionary.com

Journal Prompts: Divinely Gifted

What is your #1 takeaway from ritual?

What did you receive?

If you were to lead this in a women's circle, how would you make this your own?

Closing Prayer

We are the only ones who can bring ourselves from darkness to light.
Wishing everyone health, love, peace, joy in harmony.
Wishing there will be peace among all people.
Wishing we find a cure for all diseases.
Wishing there will be no more suffering in the world.
Take this peaceful moment, spread it and share it with our family, friends and strangers.
Om Shanti, Shanti, Om. Peace, Peace, Peace.
Namaste.

Gratitude Gift

Design Your Goddess Lifestyle Planner

https://www.goddesslifestyleplan.com/design-your-goddess-lifestyle-planner/

Want to live an abundant life of happiness, success and fulfillment?

This fabulous planner will show you step-by-step **how to design a custom goddess lifestyle** that gratifies your unique passions, desires and needs!

The Design Your Goddess Lifestyle Planner™ Will:

- Get you crystal clear on your desires and needs.
- Identify what "things" have been missing from your life.
- Unearth your hidden desires.
- Activate your purpose.
- Make your life juicer than you thought possible.
- Inspire the shit out of you!

> We are the only ones who can bring ourselves from darkness to light.

Lisa Marie Grantham Lisa Marie Grantham is best known as the founder of The Goddess Lifestyle Plan®. An intuitive entrepreneur, Lisa helps conscious women build, scale, and leverage a profitable online business and design an abundant lifestyle they love by working in harmony with nature, the Universe, and the elemental forces of creation so they can enjoy a life filled with passion, purpose, and prosperity!

On a mission to bring esoteric wisdom out of the closet and into the mainstream, Lisa has found that living in flow with nature's rhythm's is an ancient and effective path for ambitious women who are ready to live life at their fullest potential. Lisa believes that the future is limitless and each of us are divine co-creator's with the Universe and that whatever happened in the past does not define your future or you.

An Elemental Priestess and practitioner of esoteric traditions, Lisa's unique combination of strategic thinking, laser sharp intuition, vast knowledge of holistic health, psychology, human behavior, and healing modalities plus 30+ years of metaphysical study and practice results in an effective mix of spirituality and "real world," no-nonsense practicality that supports her students and private clients in embracing their own Inner Goddess.

When she's not teaching, coaching or whipping up herbal lotions, potions and herbal remedies, Lisa loves spending time with her husband Shannon boating around the Gulf Of Mexico, visiting her children and grandchildren in New York, and taking care of her menagerie of furred, feathered, and scaled animal companions living at Bokee Farm, their tropical farm located on a barrier island off the coast of SW Florida. https://www.goddesslifestyleplan.com/

Made in the USA
Middletown, DE
15 May 2023